This Old Building

*A Guide to Buying, Restoring, and
Managing Historic Commercial Property*

Robert K. Hall

This Old Building

   – A Guide to Buying, Restoring, and Managing Historic Commercial Property
by Robert K. Hall

ISBN-13: 978-0692635063
ISBN-10: 0692635068

Daylight Properties
1155 North State Street
Bellingham, WA 98225

Daylightproperties.com

Editor and Contributing Writer: Kendra Langeteig
Book Design and Typesetting: Kate Weisel
Front Cover Photo: Kane Hall
Front Cover Design: May May Gong
Author Photo: Peter James

Dedication

Anything of enduring value can never really be owned, a person can only take care of it for awhile and then pass it on, hopefully in even better shape than when you got it. This is especially true of historic buildings.

In light of this, I would like to dedicate this book to the memory of all the original builders and owners of these historic buildings.

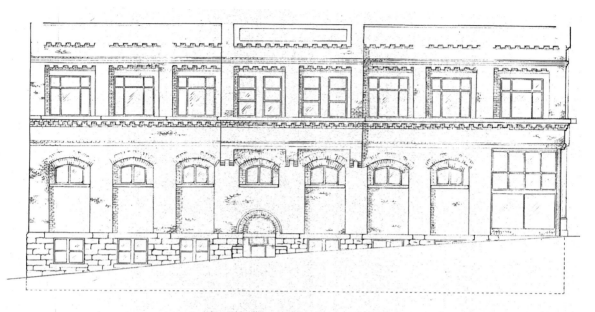

CHESTNUT STREET ELEVATION

STATE STREET ELEVATION SCALE ¼" = 1'

Robert Hall

Architectural drawing of the Daylight Building by Robert Hall.

Contents

Introduction

PART ONE

The Joys and Pains of Restoring Old Buildings

Commercial Warehouse

Classic Small Hotel

Arts & Crafts Apartment Building

General Supply Store

One-Story Retail Building

Society Clubhouse

PART TWO

The Nuts 'n Bolts of the Old Building Business

Acknowledgements

THIS BOOK HAD BEEN SHAPING in my mind for years before I sat down to write about my adventures with old buildings. I am grateful to my editor Kendra Langeteig, who encouraged me to finally commit my story to paper. Without her expert writing support and editorial work, this book would not have been possible.

The historic photographs in this book go a long way in telling the story of these old buildings. I want to express my appreciation to Jeff Jewell, Archivist, Whatcom Museum, for his assistance with photos of the Bellingham properties. I also wish to thank to Chris Moore, Executive Director, Washington Trust for Historic Preservation; Jeff Creighton, Archivist, Northwest Museum of Arts and Culture; and Andy Skinner, Museum Director, Lewis County Historical Museum; for their assistance with historic photos of the properties in Spokane and Chehalis.

Kane Hall, my son and partner, made valuable comments on book drafts and assisted in selecting photography. Special thanks to my business partner David Johnston for contributing photographs of our projects. Special thanks to Kane Hall, Jason Koski, Dal Neitzel, Kate Weisel, and Peter James for their photography. Jeff Stiles deserves mention for his editorial support with the finance chapter. Thank you to Kate Weisel for her book design and typesetting.

Photographer: Peter James

Foreword

Ever dream of buying an old building and fixing it up, but you didn't know where to start? *This Old Building* will give you a wealth of information and practical advice on how to purchase and finance a restoration project, as well as how to deal with the inevitable surprises inherent in any historic building restoration. The book also provides guidance on how to manage a building once it has been restored, and to successfully earn a living from leasing its commercial and residential space.

Robert Hall shares first-hand experience from almost 30 years of buying, rehabilitating, renting, and managing historic buildings. Hall's engaging stories of how he got started in the "rehab" business show how much has changed since the 1980s when he had to finance his first project himself. Back then, banks were not interested in loaning money to restore an abandoned building in a downtown that was experiencing increased vacancy. Readers will learn from the risks Hall took and mistakes he made over the years, experience that can be expensive to come by for the novice building rehabber.

This Old Building has just the right mix of how-to plus personal experience to give the reader confidence to undertake their own restoration project. The book excels in giving a comprehensive overview of situations that often arise in the process, with photos of buildings that Hall brought back to life.

Robert Hall's contribution cannot be overemphasized. Without his proactive vision and unfaltering determination, downtown Bellingham would not look as it does today. Where many saw derelict buildings to be torn down, Hall saw history, beauty, and opportunity. His willingness to take investment risks has brought new vitality to previously lifeless streets. Hall has tirelessly encouraged the City to adopt flexible historic building codes, and has advocated for a historic district. Leading by example, he has inspired others to invest in the downtown. Hall's work will be an inspiration to everyone who reads this book.

Kathryn Franks, Development Specialist
City Hall, Bellingham, Washington

State Street (Elk Street) in downtown Bellingham in 1926 was a thriving place with blocks of stores, hotels, and businesses convenient to the trolley lines. J. W. Sandison collection, courtesy of Whatcom Museum.

Facing page: The Daylight Building at the corner of State and Chestnut in downtown Bellingham.

Introduction

Saving Old Buildings:
Reviving the Heart of Our Cities

Back in the 1920s, Frank Lloyd Wright once said, "The outcome of the city will depend upon the race between the automobile and the elevator—and anyone who bets on the elevator is crazy." It took less than half a century for Wright's prediction about the future of our American cities to prove correct. Thanks to the automobile and the freeway, the vision of high-rise urban development with dense pedestrian-oriented centers gave way to urban sprawl, and the original footprint of towns and cities across the country expanded miles outward. Most urban centers lost not only their largest retailers, but also

The Merton Building, designed by architects Herman Preusse and Charles Carson, was built in downtown Spokane in 1890. The building was demolished in 2004 to make way for urban renewal. The entire block of historic architecture adjoining the Merton was destroyed as well. Photos courtesy of Washington Trust for Historic Preservation.

their cultural mainstays—from theaters and nightclubs to the social clubs and hotels. Once thriving urban communities were left pocketed with abandoned and derelict buildings. Many of the old commercial buildings in those blighted neighborhoods—even buildings still viable for restoration—have been torn down, often to make space for parking lots. Old buildings that escaped demolition sit vacant or underused and in a state of disrepair—or worse, defaced by some poorly conceived modernization scheme.

In the name of progress, we have destroyed much of the historic architecture that connects us with our past. This is a great loss to our American cities. But it's not too late to reverse the trend. In fact, many historic commercial properties have been brought back into full use by developers like myself, who recognize their cultural importance as well as their great investment potential. While most people are inclined to look at an old building and see a pile of junk that blights the neighborhood, I always look for the opportunity to restore a dying building back to life. When renovated, these buildings revive the urban community by providing attractive commercial/residential space, and give people a connection with our cultural heritage that can't be found in a suburban shopping mall.

During the past twenty-five years, I have purchased and restored more than thirty historic commercial buildings in the state of Washington, primarily in Bellingham, where I have focused my redevelopment efforts. My career began almost by accident when I purchased my first old building as a warehouse for my import business, without giving much thought to its historic value. Getting inside that building gave me my first taste of the joy of restoration. I dusted off a century of use, uncovered the original underlying structure, and made the building fit to last another 100 years. Through trial and error, I have developed a system for efficiently renovating these historic commercial buildings, along with practical solutions for managing and financing this property to make it profitable. Without good strategy for rehabbing a building to get a bottom-line profit margin, a restoration project could turn out to be a work in progress that never gets finished. If done with foresight and deliberation, however, these buildings will be given a new extended life that provides the owner with a reliable income and gives the community a restored heritage building.

My mission to save old buildings was sparked as an architectural engineering student at Washington State, when I left school to study the historic architecture of Europe and Asia. It was during this trip in 1969 that I came to appreciate the basic design principles that make the pre-1930s buildings in our cities so worth the time and effort to preserve. I rode the Orient Express from Milan through Eastern Europe to Istanbul, and traveled by bus and train to Tehran, Lahore, New Delhi, Bombay, and Katmandu, and back overland to Europe. From Greece, I hitchhiked through Europe, visiting the capitol cities as well as small cities and towns. I became fascinated with the construction of the old commercial buildings in these cities. These buildings were built to last for many generations, unlike the products of modern construction practices, noted for quick and easy applications and shoddy materials designed for the short term.

The historic buildings that anchor the centers of the smaller European towns seemed to have existed in a timeless way for hundreds of years. I was especially curious at that time to find out how a building built over 500 years ago could still be functioning. In Bern, Switzerland, the majority of the downtown architecture was built before Christopher Columbus set sail for America. The buildings in Bern are protected by city code, which forbids the owners of these properties to change any exterior features, not even the color, though it allows them to modernize the interior to keep current with mechanical and aesthetic trends.

While studying these historic buildings, I was struck by the fact that the older commercial buildings of Europe looked almost exactly like the older buildings in our American cities—from Boston or Atlanta to Seattle and San Diego—

Photographer: Cristo Vlahos.

Historic street in Bern, Switzerland, virtually unchanged for hundreds of years.

in terms of their size, design, and material, even though our buildings were built hundreds of years after their European cousins in wildly varying geographic locations. This resemblance comes down to the fundamental design principles of this architecture, which was based on the resources available for construction and the practical needs of people living in an urban setting.

The builders of historic commercial structures followed a standard practice of building one to three stories high, often with a basement below street level for storage. The interior proportions were consistent as well, from the width, height, and depth of the structure to the size of the windows and doors. This standard evolved from the nature of the materials used for construction: heavy timbers

and masonry of either brick or stone. Due to the constraints of these materials, the builders could modify the basic design features only so much. The commercial buildings were the workhorses of the towns. They were built strong with few frills, except perhaps for decorative features on the façade overlooking the street. The quality of the construction of these buildings made them fit to last for generations. They stood as a monument to the original owner and architect, and were a source of civic pride.

When I returned to the states, I was disturbed by the fact that so many fine old buildings in our American towns and cities have been lost to the forces of modernization. To see these once proud structures in the geographic center of nearly every town, village, and city abandoned and in a state of disrepair, or to look at a historic photo and see the anchor buildings that once stood on the corner now replaced by a drive-through bank teller, struck me as a terrible loss. The buildings that still survived were in danger of being vandalized by landlords, with the help of architects and their modernizing schemes.

Visiting the ancient site of Pompeii some years later, I realized that the fundamental design principles we see in the structures of Europe and America's older buildings have been used by builders for many millennia, not just the last 400 years. They were not the product of one architect or historical period, but evolved slowly, and were improved upon little by little as needs arose throughout the centuries.

The standard used for the commercial buildings pre-dating modernization in our American cities follows the same basic footprint as the commercial/residential structures of Pompeii. The ground floor merchant shops facing the street spanned no more than 25 feet wide with a depth up to 120 feet in length. Twenty-five feet is about the length a timber beam must be to serve as a floor or roof joist. A depth of 120 feet is about as long as a building can be and still get outside light to reach the interior from the front and back of the building. The ceiling height on the ground floor was 16 to 20 feet, which allowed a clearstory window to be built

> ...the fundamental design principles we see in the structures of Europe and America's older buildings have been used by builders for many millennia.

above the entrance, and gave the space enough headroom to build two stories in the back. The mezzanine in the back third of the building was adjacent to an alley, which enabled the shop and basement to be accessed for deliveries and services. The mezzanine featured windows on both floors to bring light into the building. The upper floor was used for offices or additional retail space, and the ground floor below the mezzanine was used for storage and/or offices.

Residential units were built above the ground floor shops, rising up three or four floors. These upper stories featured window wells to let in natural light and air ventilation, and often were designed with a skylight to allow light to penetrate the middle of the retail space. One must remember that these buildings evolved long before the invention of electricity. Lighting up a dark space with oil or candlelight was not only expensive, but also dangerous, which made natural light and airflow a major design consideration. Most of the historic cities throughout the world continue to function effectively with blocks of buildings designed to accommo-

The old buildings that survive in our American cities call out to us to rescue them from neglect or disfigurement and restore them back to life.

date retail space on the ground floor and residential housing above.

These blocks of buildings of approximately 400 to 600 ft. by 200 to 250 ft. were intersected by an alley, which allowed for delivery of goods and removal of trash. This grid system was designed to accommodate two rows of buildings with 16 to 20 retail shops lining the street. Each shop had about 25 feet of storefront facing a pedestrian sidewalk, which proved ideal for window shopping. It would take five minutes to walk the entire block while enjoying the window displays. This practical and pleasurable design for urban living grew obsolete when commerce shifted from the city centers to the suburbs, and automobiles and highway systems replaced the streetcars and trolley lines.

With the advent of steel, concrete, electricity, central heating, and elevators, all at about the same time, the aesthetic features that give old buildings their distinctive character fell out of favor. These modern innovations transformed the way architects approached building design.

Electric lighting eliminated the need for high ceilings with clearstory windows, skylights, and large windows, which came to be regarded as old-fashioned and impractical. The integrity of pre-1930's buildings was compromised when adapting the architecture to modern life, as retrofitting them with the new appliances presented insurmountable mechanical problems. Lower ceilings became the modern look, a modernization that unfortunately continues to dominate design. With the new engineering technology, straight steel I-beams and girders replaced the high-arched stone facades, as it was no longer necessary for architects to observe height restrictions and proportions based on stress loads as when designing traditional buildings.

Once architects were freed from the constraints imposed by the use of wood and brick, they began to experiment with innovative designs afforded by mass-produced materials. The buildings constructed after 1930 were often products of the imagination of architects and tradesmen open to the various interpretations of design these new materials allowed. Although the breakthrough in modern technology revolutionized construction, it also made possible a lot of ridiculous building designs.

The modern look became so widely accepted in America as a sign of progress that architects avoided designing buildings with features that resembled traditional structures. The prevailing theme in modern design has seemed to be "anything but the traditional." It was this attitude that led to many grand old buildings being replaced by modern skyscrapers or defaced in some modernization project. The buildings being built today, with the exception of some municipal structures, have a projected life expectancy of only 50 years. When a historic building is carefully rehabilitated and well maintained, it will be standing long after all of the buildings currently under construction have been torn down.

The old buildings that survive in our American cities call out to us to rescue them from neglect or disfigurement and restore them back to life. As I will demonstrate in this book with my own restoration projects, these buildings make great candidates for rehabilitation. Their timber-frame and masonry core gives this durable architecture a built-in footprint that lends itself to adapting to our current commercial/residential needs. Rehabbing an old building is also a cost effective and "green" solution, when compared with constructing a building with newly manufactured materials—not to mention the environmental cost of dumping thousands of tons of demolition waste into the landfill.

While the process of restoring a historic building is by no means a quick and easy job, it is far easier and more affordable than many of you would imagine. *This Old Building* gives you my trade secrets and best practices from years of restoration work. This is not a preservation handbook in the usual sense of restoring a building down to every architectural detail. A quality historic restoration need not involve a full-scale custom rehab, which would require a huge budget for architects, contractors, and materials. This misconception keeps many viable old buildings sitting vacant on the market that could otherwise be put to good use and provide an income stream for the investor. There's another way to save old buildings—an affordable practical alternative that does not compromise the integrity of the original architecture, and assures the property owner's success by focusing on the profit margin.

This is the book I wished to have had when starting my first rehab project. It is my hope that the stories and advice in this book will inspire many of you to become an owner and restorer of old buildings yourself—and also grow prosperous doing so! With your help, many more of these unique treasures can be preserved for future generations to enjoy.

Facing page: The arch of the demolished St. Edward Church in Shelton, Washington; an early work of architect Paul Thiry. Built in 1931; demolished in 2009.

PART ONE

The Joys and Pains of Restoring Old Buildings

Looking southeast over the Daylight Building and the Herald Building toward a South Hill neighborhood.

Learning the Trade

RESTORING HISTORIC commercial buildings was not a common practice in the 1980s when I started out on my journey. Few people wanted to invest in this property, let alone take on the challenge of rehabbing a building that had fallen into disuse. The trend in American cities was to let these old workhorses go to ruin, despite the historic importance of these buildings and their potential to boost the urban economy. At best, these commercial buildings were falling into the hands of developers who exploited them for their historic character, but often sacrificed the architecture's integrity. It is not unusual to find a building with a restored façade and a gutted and remodeled interior. Even worse are the renovations in which most of the building has been completely modernized over the years. Once I got into this line of work, I vowed to rescue as many of these old buildings as possible, so that I could bring them back to their original design and thus revive the historic element of the downtown business district.

In this first part of the book, I'll take you behind the scenes to illustrate some important lessons I learned over the years while buying, fixing up, and managing these old buildings. By taking a scaled-down, low profile approach to restoration, and leasing units while the rehab was in progress, I discovered that investing in historic commercial real estate was not only satisfying, from an urban renewal and historic perspective, but also profitable beyond my wildest dreams.

Most of the featured projects are located in Bellingham, where I have focused my redevelopment efforts, though I also include a few properties in Spokane and Chehalis. This selection of buildings gives you a cross-section of the typical commercial structures built in American cities from the 1890s to the 1920s. Each building is unique, with its own character-defining features based on the popular styles used by builders and architects. Taken as a whole, these buildings tell the story of an earlier time in history when they played a central role in the lives of citizens. As you'll see in the following chapters, these heritage buildings can continue to play an important role when they're restored back to life and repurposed to meet the changing needs of our communities.

Thiel and Welter furniture warehouse on Unity Street in Bellingham, 1935. Photograph courtesy of Whatcom Museum.

Breaking into the
Historic Restoration Business

Unity Building (1912)

115 Unity Street

Bellingham, Washington

DOWNTOWN BELLINGHAM was full of vacant or partially empty commercial buildings in 1989 when I was searching for a warehouse for my business. At that time, I was importing hand-knit sweaters from Ecuador and the inventory had outgrown my garage. Bellingham had followed the trend and constructed a large regional mall outside the city. The opening of this new retail center in 1988 resulted in an exodus of businesses from the downtown area. All of the major department stores—Bon Marche, Nordstrom, Place Two, JC

Photographer: Peter James

Bellingham from the harbor.

If you oversee the rehab process, as I have done with all of my building projects since this first one, you'll get to know your building from the inside out, and you'll save yourself a lot of money by not having to hire outside contractors to do the work.

Penney, Woolworth's and Sears, to name a few—relocated to the 800,000-sq.-ft. Bellis Fair Mall. The family-run retail stores downtown were losing their customers so rapidly that many of the owners decided it was prime time to close business or move to a strip mall. With the vacant buildings transforming Bellingham into a ghost town, property values began to plummet and commercial real estate went up for sale cheaply. Needless to say, it was a buyer's market.

There were brick buildings with great historic character on the market, but in view of Bellingham's geographic location in an earthquake zone, I was frightened of owning a brick structure. Instead, I found an unsexy, box-shaped concrete building on Unity Street that looked like a good candidate. Back then, I wasn't thinking in terms of buying an old building as an investment property. I simply wanted a well-built structure to serve as a warehouse.

Henry Thiel and Joseph Welter constructed the building in 1912 to stock furniture for their downtown retail store. It later served as a paint store, and was also used at one time to store brown sugar. I discovered this history when the roof leaked and a sticky molasses substance dripped through the ceiling of the second floor. Above the retail space on the ground floor were two floors of warehouse space, each 110 ft. x 55 ft., connected by a set of stairs, and an old-fashioned freight elevator with wood-slat doors. The building was homely, but it had character.

The owner of the Unity Building was planning to move his bookstore on the ground floor to a strip mall, so he was eager to sell the property to me. Because the banks refused to loan money for investing in downtown real estate, the owners of Bellingham's commercial buildings were willing to sell their property for a small down payment and carry the remainder on private contracts. This meant that no bank appraisal was needed to close the deal on the Unity Building. In hindsight, I paid too much for the property: $275,000, with a $75,000 down payment from a refinance loan on my home. By comparison, the second property I purchased in Bellingham, the Helena Building on Railroad Avenue, for which I paid $180,000 with no down payment, was located in the center of the hot new retail sector. With my first building purchase, I also didn't have the foresight to see any potential rehab issues.

I was so thrilled at the prospect of owning such a large building that, in my excitement, I forgot to check the city records on the property. Had I done so, I would have learned that the previous owner had been working on improvements in the building without a permit. Even more inexcusable, the city building department caught and red tagged them, which meant they had to halt the work and get a permit. Because I had purchased the property from the owner with a private contract, no appraisal was required for the sale. If a bank had been involved, this information would have been discovered and prevented the deal from closing. As it was, the two realtors involved in the sale (including my agent) were looking at their shared 5% commission and didn't want to call attention to anything that might stop the deal from going through.

When the property came into my possession, the city building department threatened to condemn the building unless I installed a one-hour, fire protected corridor with a rear exit that connected with the second and third floors. This code upgrade had to be designed and built quickly. So not only had I acquired a warehouse, but I also had my first historic rehab suddenly handed to me. This gave me my first shot at being resourceful when dealing with restoration issues. I would soon learn that, like it or not, the best plan for rehabbing a building and making a profit is to do as much of the work as possible yourself.

As it turned out, I was uniquely qualified to deal with the rehab issues in my first building. After studying architectural engineering for four years, I knew how to

Photographer: David H. Johnston

The Unity Building is an example of the functional style popular for commercial warehouses in the early 20th century.

draw up the floor plans for a rehab. The city accepted my architectural drawings and plans for the Unity project without a hitch, as there was no need for an official architect's stamp at that time. Today, to renovate a building in Bellingham of over several thousand square feet the owner is required to have an architect involved in the project. To rehab the Unity building, I also had previous years of experience as a carpenter and a working knowledge of all the trades, from electrical wiring to plumbing. I had already rehabbed many houses and built my own house in Hawaii with the help of my father. Even coming in with skills, most of what I now know about this trade I had to learn on the job. Back then, I wasn't able to anticipate the kind of improvements an old building like the Unity might need or the expenses potentially involved in the restoration.

Rehab projects like these can take many years to complete.

Because of the inherited stop-work orders on the building and the work required by the city to be performed for the rehab, I did not have the luxury of time. If I wanted to succeed in completing this project and not lose the building to condemnation, I needed cash. So right away, I was in a financial bind, because banks were not loaning money on commercial buildings. The only solution was to use the $50,000 line of credit reserved for my import business, along with the balance on my credit card. This pressured me to sell my house a year later to pay back the line of credit that comes due every year. To avoid paying any rent during this transition, I moved my family of two boys into the top floor of the Unity Building. For over a year, we essentially camped out in the building, sleeping on foam pads and cooking on a camp stove.

The restoration work was completed slowly over a period of two years. I worked on renovations in my spare time while continuing to run my import business. Though it can be frustrating to make such slow progress, it has the benefit of giving you the time to make wise decisions. The project initially involved dividing up the building's two huge 6,000 sq. ft. spaces into five smaller more easily rentable spaces, and putting in a rear exit to meet safety regulations.

When I ran out of money for further renovations, I learned how to apply for various Community Development Loans.

The city anticipated losing downtown business to the mall when it opened, and had the foresight to reserve funds to help finance urban restoration projects such as mine. With one loan, I financed the façade improvement, which enabled me to paint the exterior. A second loan covered the cost of improving the rear exit. A licensed contractor completed this work quickly. When the Unity project was finally completed after two long years, and I received my occupancy permit from the city, I swore that never again would I get involved in the restoration of an old building.

I located a realtor to rent out the newly renovated spaces in the Unity Building while my children and I enjoyed a three-month, work related vacation in Ecuador. When we returned, I discovered that only the original ground floor tenant was paying rent; the five new spaces remained just as I had left them—unoccupied. The realtor explained that he had put a sign in one of the windows, but that nobody called to inquire. "The downtown is dead," he said. Then and there, I decided to become a realtor with a small "r," meaning not licensed. It is legal to lease and sell your own properties. To attract tenants, I had a sign company make two giant 6-ft. x 12-ft. banners and hung them from the sides of the building. I was prepared to lease the space to any tenant with any kind of business, and within four months, the building was fully rented.

The downtown area of Bellingham was so depressed by the loss of its retail and office tenants that nobody besides me was willing to take a risk and convert the space of these empty buildings. Bank loans for downtown development were available only as a Small Business Loan guaranteed by the federal government, and eligibility was limited to people whose business was located in their building. That gave me a corner on the market, as I provided some of the only new and hip loft-style spaces in town. For the Unity Building, I was able to tap into the community development funds and façade loans available through the city to complete the project.

Once we finished the rehab, the Unity Building filled to capacity with tenants. We had a bookstore on the ground floor; a children's theater, a Christian youth center, and my warehouse on the second floor; and a video production company and a Buddhist meditation center on the top floor. The building was full and vibrant and, I might add, continues to be to this day.

After the third year of owning this building, I was shocked to see on my annual tax return that the building had made a profit of over $35,000, and that profit was tax free, due to tax credits earned through the historic rehab and depreciation. In this case, it was a 10% tax credit based on the total cost of the project, which more than covered all my Federal income tax for that year. In fact, I would not have to pay any Federal Income tax for the next 20 years. When I saw this profit on my tax return, and not having to

> It is far more profitable to keep your building and recapture your investment with refinance, because after the rehab you know everything about the structure and the neighborhood. You have a feel for the whole building, from the mechanical side to the right tenants for it.

pay 30% of the total to the government, I quickly reconsidered my pledge not to do any more rehabs.

The Unity Building is one of the few properties that I've sold, after owning it for over 12 years. Even back then, I realized that it's not wise to sell your property. But the learning curve was so great with this first project that looking at it even today brings up painful associations. I was happy to let this one go. I sold it to one of the tenants on the second floor for $950,000 and used the profit to buy a building in another city, the Mottman Building in Olympia, Washington, about the same size as the Unity Building but of far greater quality.

For those of you who want to get into the old building business, my advice is to be as hands-on as possible to make your investment pay off. With the right information up front and careful strategy throughout the process, you can avoid some of the painful mistakes I made with my first restoration project.

The Helena Hotel on Railroad Avenue, c. 1928. The 20-room hotel spanned the second floor above the retail shops on the street level. Photograph courtesy of Whatcom Museum.

Reformed Character:
From Flophouse to Street-Side Charmer

Helena Building/Helena Hotel (1908)
1313-1315 Railroad Avenue
Bellingham, Washington

RAILROAD AVENUE was the first street in downtown Bellingham to recover vitality after the Bellis Fair Mall opened north of the city in 1988. The avenue runs four city blocks, with two abandoned railroad tracks running through the middle of the street, and two one-way streets on either side. Freight cars originally parked on the tracks to unload merchandise, primarily food products for wholesale and retail, into the warehouse buildings alongside the tracks. The entire four blocks were lined with shops in an open-air public market. People would come down on the electric trolley line from all over the city to buy their groceries and supplies. The train tracks were removed in the mid-1970s to make room for parking on all four blocks. Railroad Avenue, and especially the 1300 block, became the first hot spot in the new downtown because of the convenient parking and rows of shops and restaurants on the street.

The Helena Building, 2015.

The Helena entrance in 1994.

In 1994, I was searching for a commercial building with space to warehouse my imports that would also provide an attractive street-level space for a retail shop. Railroad Avenue was the first place I looked. The historic Helena Building on the 1300 block seemed like the perfect candidate. At that point in time, the Helena Building was considered to be the most run-down property in the downtown district, though it was quite a contest, as there were many contenders—especially the Flame Tavern across the street, long since shut down as a public nuisance. The Helena was the classic dream property. It was the worst building in the best location.

The owner of the Helena Building was an elderly gentleman in his eighties who had inherited the property from his father. When I approached him about renting the space, it was in such bad shape that he said he would let me have it for two years, rent-free, if I fixed it up. I was well aware of how much work it would take to do the job, so I politely asked if he would sell me the property. I remember how his eyes lit up. Without hesitating, he nodded. Apparently, he was embarrassed at how far this once proud building had fallen since the days when his father ran a successful plumbing business in the building. The price was $180,000 with only closing cost down, a reasonable price; but the cost of the total project seemed beyond my means at the time. He was happy to sell me the building at a discount and carry a 5-year mortgage on the total price of the property, provided I fixed up the building to protect his capital by investing my time and money in the rehab. The fact that I had successfully completed a rehab just one block away convinced him that I could handle the work.

We walked through the building together to look at its potential for retail and warehouse space. The Helena Building actually comprises two separate buildings that were combined in the 1920s to create a 20-room hotel on the second floor. The original twenty rooms of the hotel had been converted into a 10-room apartment building. This conversion was necessary because modern building codes required two forms of egress, and ten of the original rooms lacked exterior windows. In this case, the hallway and an exterior window provided the forms of egress. Windows are suitable for the first two stories, but a separate corridor or exterior fire escape is required for higher stories.

The owner declined to go upstairs to view the leased apartment space. "It's a boar's nest up there," he said. The owner hadn't been upstairs for years, as he leased the entire top-floor hotel space to a tenant who subleased the other units. The total rent collected from these ten apartments when I purchased the building amounted to a mere $400 per month. So you can imagine the deplorable condition of the units at the time. In addition to the apartment space, there were two shared bathrooms and a small business office on the second floor.

Looking through the office files, I came across receipts dating back to the 1950s when the Helena served as a transient hotel. Rooms were rented for as little as $5 a night. The Beat poet Gary Snyder mentions the Helena Hotel in his poem, "Night Highway Ninety Nine." He stayed at the hotel while en route to a summer job at a fire lookout in the forests of the Cascade Mountains. We can assume that Snyder's friend Jack Kerouac, of *On the Road* fame, stayed at the Helena as well, since he also took a job at the lookout that summer.

On the street level beneath the hotel, there was a notorious bar called the Shenandoah, with a card room in the back. Over the years, the bar expanded into the three adjoining retail spaces on the ground floor to take over the entire

The Helena Building has a colorful history. The hotel was used at one time as a brothel. A court record from the 1920s shows furniture from the hotel sold at auction to pay the tax levied on "houses of ill repute." The tax revenue collected from such places went toward funding the schools and the fire and police departments. Bellingham, like other western cities at that time, had a lot of hard-working, unmarried men living in town who worked in the logging, mining, and fishing industries, as well as the mills and canneries. On weekends, the town filled up with these workers looking for entertainment and a place to sleep. Cheap hotels and bordellos were scattered across town to accommodate them.

space of over 5,000 sq. ft. The Shenandoah had been closed for several years when I found the building. The police department explained that it had become a public nuisance like the tavern across the street. The situation got so bad that I was told by the police that this space could never again be used for a bar establishment, although now after 20 years, I think it could.

Removing brick to expose the original windows facing the alley.

To rehab this derelict building and revive the architecture would present some challenges. Two layers of hung ceilings covered the original one, and two layers of stud walls were built over the original brick wall. Ironically, the finish on the walls of the main room was cheap red vinyl wallpaper with an antique brick design, which looked just like the original brick wall that had been covered up with plaster. The floors of the retail spaces were off by up to three inches and would have to be leveled.

I drew up my own schematic plans to get the building permit. I planned to strip the interiors to the exposed ceiling rafters and brick walls, leaving only the supporting walls. Once that was done, I wanted to fix any structural problems and replace windows that had been removed over the years to give the new retail spaces plenty

of street exposure and natural light. Upstairs in the hotel space, I planned to rebuild all of the rooms and bathrooms and put in a laundry facility for the residents. This basic step-by-step plan we used for renovating the Helena building became our standard procedure for rehabbing buildings.

By the time I acquired this building, I knew what I was doing as far as financing a long-term rehab project. I also understood the importance of being as resourceful and hands-on as possible to stretch my budget. I applied for two HUD loans and received $70,000 to renovate the ground floor and $15,000 for the façade. The following year, I received an additional $70,000 HUD loan for the upstairs renovation. So the entire budget was $170,000, about $25 per sq. ft.—not much, considering that this figure included the cost of four new heating systems and three new bathrooms on the main floor.

While waiting for the loans to be approved, the first thing I did was to cover up the front of the building to protect the original building while we worked on the renovation. Besides the need to keep dust and noise from the sidewalk, I did not want any inquisitive people poking around the project to interrupt our progress. I especially did not want to attract any undue attention from city officials who might require me to get special permits to complete costly upgrades that would involve hiring an engineer. It's easy to take care of straightforward mechanical issues right away without hiring a contractor.

Old commercial buildings have a basic timber-frame structure with standard proportions that makes it possible to rehab most any building. But each building has its own unique issues after years of different ownership. Makeshift improvements and alterations often compromise the integrity of the building. Because the Helena Building was constructed by combining two buildings, one of the staircases to the second floor hotel had been removed. The owner or contractor who removed the stairs had sup-

Saving the bones of the Helena Hotel.

ported the floor joists with a wooden beam made of many pieces of wood haphazardly nailed together. The beam, which ran the full 25-foot width of the retail space, was covered up when the ceiling was lowered. I resolved this issue by cutting a hole in the floor under the original stairs, pouring a concrete footing, and installing a metal post up to the joist header to support it, as in the original construction of the building in 1908. I made sure to add a patina to the beam to make it look original. We succeeded in restoring the architectural character. Unfortunately, due to the alteration of the original design, the Helena Building would not be a candidate for the National Register despite its historic interest.

To level the uneven floors of the retail spaces, I hired a contractor to do the job. His solution was to pour a layer of light-weight concrete over the glued down carpets and floor tiles, and float it evenly

The Helena façade, given a new art deco theme.

across the surface. I did not approve of this method at the time, but after twenty years of regular use, it still seems to be working well.

The original front of the building had been boarded up with plywood when the building was vacated. Replacing the windows helped to bring the building back to its original appearance. We used two large 5 x 12-foot plate-glass windows that I inherited from a contractor who had remodeled a mall store. Windows of this size are expensive and heavy, and I was fortunate that these replacements worked perfectly for the Helena Building.

In retrospect, I probably did not need to be so stealthy about making these improvements, but as a result, it all went smoothly and quickly, without any delays caused by engineering contractors requiring special permits. After I received the demo permit, I put together a low-budget crew. One of the upstairs tenants agreed to drive his truck to the dump in exchange for gas and a six-pack of beer. I hired college friends of my son Kane to gut the interior and haul the waste material to the dump. We had to work quickly, because once the loans were approved, I would be required by law to hire a licensed contractor who would have to pay "prevailing wages" of at least $28 per hour to any workers on the project. One of the conditions of these federally funded loans is that a licensed contractor has to do the job, and he has to pay the set wage. On the plus side, the job gets done quickly and by highly skilled professionals. On the down side, the cost is high and the owner loses control over the job.

The ground floor was in such terrible shape that nothing but the beer coolers could be salvaged, which made the decision to remove the rest easy. I recycled the glass beer coolers by converting them into display cabinets for jewelry. Most of the old buildings I have renovated were filled with all types of stuff that needed removal. And in the end, almost all of it ended up in a landfill. Recycling centers will generally accept used building material and things that you find in abandoned buildings, such as old appliances. Sometimes recycling facilities even pay for recyclable items and have them removed from your property at their own expense. After years of moving this stuff from one old building to the next, waiting to find a place or use for it, I have learned to follow a simple rule of thumb: *When in doubt, throw it out.*

The Helena Building had blighted the avenue for so many years that I decided to splurge on the façade to give it an art deco look. I spent the entire $15,000 on custom-made Spanish tiles to cover the exterior façade of the building below the awning. I wanted to transform this ugly

Tile being applied to the new entrance.

New steel wall studs are installed to define the retail spaces.

The award-winning façade of the restored Helena Building.

Avenue Bread, an artisan bakery and restaurant, moved into the larger space. The Radio Museum and a clothing store filled the other two spaces. One of the reasons these retail spaces rented so easily was that I had taken the time to give the façade an eye-catching, upscale appeal.

The hotel rooms rented out quickly as well, because I kept the rate low. The Helena still has some of the least expensive rooms in town. At first, I was afraid to manage an old hotel with a reputation as a flophouse. But I learned that by keeping the building clean and managing it properly, these upstairs hotel units can be real moneymakers. It is gratifying to be able to offer affordable rooms in a building with true historic character in the center of town. Staying overnight on Railroad Avenue gives people a taste of Bellingham's history, not to mention the convenience of being able to walk downstairs to the shops and restaurants on the street.

After we finished the Helena Building restoration, I received an award from the Bellingham Municipal Arts Commission for contributing to the arts in the community by restoring the building and uplifting the Railroad Avenue neighborhood. I was starting to realize that I had found a new profession, one in which I could make money as a developer and help to revitalize the historic downtown at the same time.

duckling into the grandest building on the block. Not only did I want to make a statement about the building and Railroad Avenue as an aspiring upscale location. I also wanted to make a positive bid for the future of the entire downtown, which suffered greatly, and continues to suffer, from an image problem. Few people were willing to take the time to renovate small retail spaces in the downtown. It was my hope that my project would kick off a new trend.

Once completed, the Helena Building was successful in attracting good tenants.

Photographer: David H. Johnston

Robert Hall with son and partner Kane Hall.

Facing page: The Metropole architecture retains all of its original charm to this day.

The Cost of a Long Distance Relationship: Rehabbing with Contractors

Metropole Apartment Building (1901)
178 ½ S. Howard Street
Spokane, Washington

T HE METROPOLE APARTMENT BUILDING in Spokane, Washington, is
one of the most beautiful buildings I have had the pleasure to buy and restore.
The Metropole is similar in scale and character to the Helena Building and our
small hotel properties in Bellingham, the Laube and the Windsor. It is another

Photographer: David H. Johnston

The street level retail space of the Metropole, spruced up with a new brick wall, restored pressed-tin ceiling, and hardwood floor.

classic example of mixed use commercial building style, featuring retail space on the ground floor and apartments on the upper floors. The Metropole was built during Spokane's most significant growth period, from 1900 to 1910, when the city gained fame as the Arts and Crafts capitol of America. Architect Charles F. White designed the building for owner Charles D. Bibbins. Its construction involved erecting three separate brick structures and joining them as a single property.

The Metropole was considered one of the finer apartment buildings in Spokane. It was somewhat lavish in comparison with the single-room occupancy hotels in the downtown. Each of the 18 units was equipped with its own kitchen and bathroom, as it catered to middle-income professionals.

The Metropole has operated continuously as an apartment building from its

construction to the present day. That was one of the major selling points for this property when my partner and I found it on the market.

The attractive façade of the Metropole building was well preserved when we purchased the property in 2005. The elaborately detailed entrance featured a leaded-glass oak framed door and an arched transom framed with tiled piers and a decorative canopy. The interior architecture of the building was also a quality design, with glazed terra cotta tile decorating the landing, and a pressed-tin ceiling in the front room. The rooms were arranged around an interior court with a central skylight. It was easy for us to restore the original features of the architecture. But unfortunately, the building had been poorly treated throughout the years. We eventually had to take on a total rehab of the property from 350 miles away. This rehab meant installing new plumbing and a new electrical and heating system. In fact, the entire mechanical portion of the building, including the sewer, was worn out.

The Metropole Apartment building was my second attempt to rehab a property using second party contractors and agents. To accomplish the restoration, we hired contractors and leasing agencies. Although this project turned out to be successful, and this particular building was a striking beauty, it will be a long time before my partner and I recapture our original investment. Working on this project long distance, we learned a

The interior hallway, with original woodwork and transom windows.

lesson about trying to restore buildings located too far away to oversee the process on a day-to-day basis. If this building rehab had not been so costly, I would have been in a position to move on many more buildings. At that time, I was looking for prospects in every town within a 500-mile radius of Bellingham, as far away as Helena, Montana.

The Metropole was a success—but just. After that experience, I curtailed my ambition, and my advice would be to avoid getting lured into a long-distance rehab project, regardless of how attractive the property may be.

General George Pickett's House in 1926 (now a museum). Photograph courtesy of Whatcom Museum.

General Supply Store

Great Character, Bad Vintage

Pickett Building (1889)
1001-1007 DuPont Street and 1609 F Street
Bellingham, Washington

THE PICKETT BUILDING was the first significant historic commercial property to come into my hands. This building is named after General George Pickett, who commanded the Fort Bellingham stockade in 1856, and later served as a Confederate General in the Civil War. It is one of the three remaining historic properties from the original town of Whatcom. The two-story brick Pickett Building was constructed in 1889 to serve as a general store.

The Pickett Building today, much as it looked in its prime.

Pickett's house was built across the street from the store, where he lived with his second wife, rumored to be a Haida Indian princess. The Pickett house was built in 1856 with lumber from the nearby Roeder-Peabody lumber mill. It is among the oldest wood structures built in the future state of Washington. The other building of historic importance in Bellingham is the brick storehouse built on its original waterfront in 1850.

> For all their historic charm, I discovered that many of these pre-1900 buildings were not built to last more than a century.

This small building, which later served as the territorial courthouse, stored supplies for miners en route to British Columbia during the Fraser River Gold Rush in 1857. During the gold rush, the population of Bellingham swelled to 10,000, declining to a population of a few hundred until the 1880s.

The owner of the Pickett building contacted me soon after I received my award for the Helena Building renovation. Almost overnight, I had become the go-to person for owners of old buildings with problems, and I attracted unhappy owners of distressed properties who wanted to get out from under them. The Pickett Building's owner was an elderly gentleman who had loaned money to a young developer to fix up his property.

The developer had a vision for this historic building, and deserves credit for commemorating General Pickett by naming it after him. Unfortunately, however, the young man was a novice at renovation. After burning up the investor's loan money, he abandoned the project and left the city, leaving the tenant in this building stranded without power.

This developer had done quite a bit of work on the building, including pouring a new concrete foundation under the building, and building out three of the four residential rental units as planned. Unfortunately, he ran into zoning problems. Because the building is not located in the downtown, he was required by law to supply parking spaces, and was one space short of the required number. Besides the difficulty of getting an occupancy permit, the money he had borrowed by that time exceeded the value of the building.

I quickly agreed to take over the project and buy the building from the owner, at a much lower value than owed, but only on the promise that he would loan me money to complete the renovation and buy the adjoining rental house. We needed this house in order to take advantage of the potential parking spaces in its backyard and get the needed occupancy permit. Also this house was in dire need of repairs and yard work. Its unsightly appearance brought down the entire block. The owner agreed to give me the loan and I was thrilled to own my first truly historic property over 100 years old.

We immediately ran into structural issues with the Pickett Building. The bricks used for construction material were inferior in quality and many had crumbled beyond the point where they could be salvaged. I discovered that duct tape was being used on the roof to hold the bricks of the parapet in place. Apparently, the bricks used for buildings during that time period were recycled ballast from the merchant vessels that sailed to the Pacific Northwest from China. Bellingham's first brick factory didn't start operation until around 1900, at which point the quality of the buildings improved dramatically. I went on to buy another historic building made with these inferior bricks, the Oakland Block, also built in 1889. After these two challenging rehab projects, I vowed not to buy another property in Bellingham built before the "modern" brick factory was in production. My rule of thumb for buying a building now is that its original timber-frame and masonry core must be structurally sound. There still are many robust old buildings on the market built strong enough to last for hundreds of years.

The Pickett Building was basically a wooden structure with a brick exterior façade, and these bricks were not hard-fired. The bricks had become so soft and porous that they could be hollowed out by hand with a coin. In the rear of the building, the bricks had bowed out from the wall to the extent that it looked as if they might collapse the supporting structure (though, in reality, the underlying wood was quite durable). This bulge was such a prominent feature of the property that a story was commonly told about the Pickett Building. According to the story, there was a safe hidden in the wall of the building that was exploded during a robbery. It was this explosion that caused the bulge in the wall.

Despite the frustration of having to work with inferior brick, as they were not structural, I was able to replace them with filler and blend it in. I went on to complete the Pickett Building renovation. We

The side exit of the Pickett Building gets a code update.

converted the space into four residential units and a retail space that would serve as the neighborhood coffee shop. I eventually sold this building because it was not well built, and I could foresee problems with it in the future. But, to this day, I feel good that I was able to complete this project. I am glad to have helped preserve this prominent building on a busy street corner that anchors this part of the town to its historic past.

Naturally, I am in favor of saving as many of these old historic buildings as possible that are fast disappearing from our cities. But I would think twice before you purchase an old building with great historic character but poor quality construction.

New façade on Cliff Barlow's leather goods store, 1925. Photograph courtesy of Whatcom Museum.

Barlow's store was stocked with quality luggage. Photograph courtesy of Whatcom Museum.

First Impressions:
You Can't Judge a Building by Its Cover

Barlow Building (1892/1925)
211 West Holly Street
Bellingham, Washington

THE BARLOW BUILDING is recognized in the National Register as one of the few well-preserved, single-storied commercial buildings of its period in Bellingham's business district. The decorative façade is typical of the Mission Revival style popular for retail commercial structures in the 1920s. The Barlow Building didn't look the way it does today when I found the building on the market. The distinctive façade was buried under layers of the pink corrugated roofing material that was commonly used to cover up old buildings in the 1960s. The building had most recently served as a hair design school until the business closed. After purchasing the property in 2000, I discovered a vintage design hidden underneath the surface while in the process of tearing off the facade. We were excited to find the original decorative detailing on the parapet and the decorative brick facing still in good condition.

The Barlow Building lived through several ownerships and architectural styles over the years. Philip Baum constructed the brick building in 1892 to serve as a grocery store. The building changed hands, but continued as a grocery store

Photographer: Jason Koski

The Barlow building, restored to life.

Pink roofing material concealed the architectural treasure hidden underneath.

His leather goods store was conveniently located on busy Holly Street, with trolley lines right outside the door to transport customers from the outer city and "street-car suburbs."

To give his modest building more visibility among the larger commercial establishments in the neighborhood, including the large hardware store next door, Barlow remodeled the façade in 1925. The façade conversion involved adding brick and marble facing, building a curved decorative parapet at the top, and installing leaded windows and display windows on the storefront.

We were fortunate to find the architecture of the building intact, except for the façade below the awning, which had been torn out, and the original marble tile entryway, which was covered by concrete. The 1960 modernization was so slapdash that the concrete could be pulled off quickly to expose not just the polished marble, but also the original foundations for the entryway display windows (see photos on pages 117 and 118). This type of defacement of an irreplaceable classic historic building by a trained architect baffles me, and it is still going on. The only possible motive could be to rebrand the structure to the new owner, as if to say, "This is my design now and my building." Usually this work was done on the cheap, and hence, parts of the original design can be used—or in this case, restored easily.

until 1907, when it was converted into the Crown Bar. This establishment was a popular watering hole until the city declared Prohibition in 1910. The building stood vacant until 1913, when Clifford Barlow purchased the property to operate a leather goods company from this space until 1959. The Barlow Building's central location in the business district contributed to Barlow's long-standing success.

Stripping away the exterior façade material. Care is taken to protect the original brick design.

To renovate the interior retail space of the building, we stripped out the stud

Photographer: Jason Koski

The Barlow holds its own on the block alongside Bellingham Hardware.

walls and removed the plaster to expose a series of curved glass windows. By opening up these windows, and uncovering the skylights and cut-glass clearstory window in front, we succeeded in transforming the space back to its bright and airy original look.

The exposed brick walls and polished wood floors give the remodeled retail space an artsy upscale look that fits the urban scene. This unique little building adds vitality to the street. The Barlow Building's first tenant when it reopened was the owner of a video store. Small structures like the Barlow Building can be found in urban communities all over America. They have great potential as investment properties and make ideal start-up projects. It's not a bad idea to get practice rehabbing a small building before you get involved in a long-term renovation on a large-scale property.

Photographer: Kane Hall

Refurbishing the original hardwood floor. The original brick surfaces lining the interior were replaced with good quality brick.

Photographer: Jason Koski

Preserved historic character blends with the Barlow's clean modern look.

Elks Hall in full regalia for the State BPOE Convention in 1915. Photograph courtesy of Whatcom Museum.

Facing page: The Elks Building, 2015.

The Greater Fool Strategy:
When to Clean It Up and Get Out

Elks Club (BPOE) Building (1912)
1414 Cornwall Avenue
Bellingham, Washington

THE ELKS CLUB BUILDING in downtown Bellingham, formerly known as the BPOE (Benevolent and Protective Order of Elks) Building, was built in 1912. Architect William Cox designed the two-story brick clubhouse in the Classical Revival style popular during that prosperous boom time in Bellingham. With its arched window wells and white columns accentuating the light brick façade, the Elks Building on Cornwall Avenue is one of the finest historic street fronts in the downtown. These clubhouse buildings were built to last

Photographer: David H. Johnston

The arched window wells and white columns accentuating the brick façade are features of Classical Revival style.

for generations. Many of them still stand as a monument to that bygone era.

Most historic downtowns in America constructed their clubhouses in the same general neighborhood. Next to and across the street from the Elks Club are two other private clubs that were built during the same era. These clubs played an important role in the life of the community. Membership in the fraternal lodges, with their elaborate initiation ceremonies and private events, gave prestige to the people who joined them. The clubhouses also served as popular venues for civic activities. The Elks Club in Bellingham was equipped with two banquet halls and a large ballroom to host large public events. The popularity of these establishments waned when local businesses moved from the urban center to suburban locations.

After the Bellis Fair Mall opened in 1988, the Elks Club Building was among the vacant buildings in the downtown district purchased by the city with the prospect of acquiring state and federal funds to rehab them. The cost estimate the city received to fix up this building was spectacular. Consequently, the building stood vacant for years, making it susceptible to damage, as nobody was assigned to oversee its maintenance. Due to condition issues in many of Bellingham's old commercial buildings, and the policy changes of the new mayor and city council, city staff was advised to sell these properties quickly. Because of my reputation as a successful redeveloper, I was selected to inherit this building from the city. I only paid $170,000 (on a 5-year mortgage with only closing costs as a down payment), which was what the city had paid for it a few years earlier.

During the two years that the city owned the property, serious neglect had taken its toll on the building. Apparently, nobody was checking on the building and the utilities had been disconnected. Pigeons were in the habit of entering through the broken windows to roost

The lodge room was reserved for private meetings and ceremonies.

indoors. Bouts of severe winter freezes had caused the roof drains to freeze, and heavy spring rains caused interior leakage. The flat roof surface collected water in a central drain that had clogged and flooded the perimeter walls, knocking out the electrical system. To add to the damage, frozen pipes had burst in several places. And yet the structure of the building was robust.

The Elks Club was built with the highest of standards. It had great finishes, such as a boardroom with a massive fireplace and paneled walls. The mahogany doors and framing of the interior rooms were in excellent condition. But it had one major problem inherent in these types of structures as far as converting them for commercial/residential use. It was not designed for retail space. These club buildings work well for conversion into nightclubs and restaurants or dance studios. Unfortunately, they often have a

major problem from a design standpoint. Typically, the floor plan doesn't meet modern ADA requirements or current fire code requirements. In this case, for example, to get to the main vestibule area, you have to walk up a half flight of stairs. This rules out the possibility of installing a window for retail space. From the landing, you can walk up a grand staircase to the spacious ballroom, or descend the stairs to the bar and game room in the daylight basement. Because of the ADA Law enacted in 1990, these upper and lower floor levels as well as the main floor could not be legally used as assembly halls as originally intended, without installing a four-stop elevator (four stops, to make it accessible from the ground level).

And to top it off, because of the extensive intact façade, the only place to put this elevator without destroying the front of the building was in the alley.

At first, I was reluctant to take on

such a large project that, to start with, would require an elevator installation. But in spite of my reservations and because the city made me an offer I couldn't refuse, I became the owner of this 18,000-sq.-ft. building. To sweeten the deal, my payments would not start for six months.

We set to work fixing the plumbing and heating in the building. By this time, I had hired a general handyman as a full-time employee. First, I had him replace all the light bulbs in the building. I went down to the electrical room and pulled the main switches to every floor. Like magic, all the lights went on. To take care of the plumbing, friends and family members posted themselves throughout the building in every bathroom and kitchen. When I turned on the main water valve for just a minute, we quickly located all the leaks. It took me only a couple of days to get

> When you get an old building into working order, it is well worth your time to list the property on the National Register.

them fixed. We now had a building with power and water. We then set about cleaning the surface damage from the pigeon debris and water leakage.

Once the Elks Building was clean and functioned mechanically, it was eligible for the National Register of Historic Places. The exterior of the building looked quite attractive from the street level with its magnificent arched windows, multi-textured bricks, and glazed terra cotta finishes. The mahogany doors and framing of the interior rooms were in excellent condition. When you get an old building like this one into working order, it is well worth your time to list the property on the National Register, as you will get an additional 10% Federal tax credit on the money spent on the rehab over the 10% already given on any building over 50 years old.

I let it be known to realtors who specialized in the downtown properties that I would be willing to sell the Elks Building to any interested party. I sold it right away to an individual who proved to be an inexperienced developer for a profit of exactly $100,000, one month before my mortgage payments were scheduled to start. The person I sold it to in 1997, who still owns this empty building, pumped hundreds of thousands of dollars into upgrades. The owner put the property on the market for an asking price of about five times what I paid for it. Because of the high price tag, this is one of the few remaining vacant buildings in the downtown. This story goes to show the importance of doing the math before you buy a property.

If you get stuck with a bad investment because you were foolish and failed to calculate the cost of renovation, you'll need to find someone more foolish than your-

The original architecture of the façade has been carefully preserved.

self to sell it to—or at least a person with more cash to invest in the rehab to make it a success. This is called the "greater fool strategy," to put it bluntly. In my case, I didn't have the money to take on the project. The sale of the Elks Club Building to recapture my investment in a refinance was absolutely crucial for my business plan at this point in time. The interest rates were well over 10% and banks simply were not giving out loans on old commercial buildings; they were divesting their portfolio of commercial property. Meanwhile, downtown Bellingham was up for sale at very low prices, almost for the price of the land less the tear down costs of the property. Owners were desperate to sell and I was desperate to buy.

With the sale of the Elks Club Building, I had $100,000 to spend. I wanted a building with a future.

It's not enough to buy an old building on the strength of its aesthetic quality or historic character—even a durable "500-year" building like the Elks Club. You have to look at the big picture to your investment. Bear in mind that commercial buildings, unlike residential property, are appraised solely on the basis of rental income. If it becomes clear that the cost of the renovation cannot be recuperated by the rental increase, the best strategy is to fix the easy stuff, clean the building, and sell it quickly for a realistic price. It's better to sell the dream than live the nightmare.

Finishing up construction of the Oakland Block with painting, 1890. The construction of trolley tracks on Holly Street was underway. Photograph courtesy of Whatcom Museum.

Changing with the Times:
The Downside to Modern Upgrades

Oakland Block (1889)
310-318 West Holly Street
Bellingham, Washington

THE OAKLAND BLOCK is a magnificent, free standing, triangular three-story building that dominates the Old Town section of Bellingham. Designed by architect Ambrose Cornwall, the architecture is typical of the early commercial style popular at the time of its construction in 1889. I purchased the Oakland Block in 1996 from a family that had owned the building for generations. Because of its age and neglected condition, the building was falling apart and the owners didn't have the motivation to restore it. As in the case of the Pickett Building, built in the same year as the Oakland, the brick structure of this building was not as robust as the buildings constructed with brick after the new factory came to town.

The Oakland Block, 2015.

The Oakland Block on Bellingham Bay, 1893. Photograph courtesy of Whatcom Museum.

Despite the obvious structural issues with the Oakland Block, its local history and prominent location in the downtown attracted me to purchase it. On the plus side, the Oakland also had five large retail stores operating on the ground floor, one of which continues to be a popular restaurant called the Old Town Café.

In 1903, the top floor of the Oakland Block temporarily served as Bellingham's first City Hall during the construction of the impressive red brick Victorian structure on a bluff overlooking the harbor. This was the year in which the towns of Whatcom, Fairhaven, and Bellingham consolidated as Bellingham to become the fourth largest city in the state of Washington. The first item on the City Council agenda was to allocate money to install ten electric light fixtures in the city offices located in the Oakland building, a new innovation at that time.

Bellingham was moving into a dramatic growth period when the modern ways were edging out the ways of the olden days. Electric streetcars were installed throughout the city, replacing the use of horses and carriages in the downtown. Maulsby's undertaking establishment located in the Oakland Block was

Maulsby's Funeral Parlors in the west side of the Oakland Block, 1905.
Photograph courtesy of Whatcom Museum.

equipped with a special electric hearse trolley to transport caskets and mourners across town to the graveyard, miles away from the funeral home. The major street improvement of electric trolley cars on Holly Street in 1907 triggered many modernizations of façades facing the street. I was surprised that these "improvements" started happening that long ago, even when the buildings were almost new. The existing wooden structures were torn down and replaced with modern brick facades featuring a new squared-off window design for commercial buildings.

The top floor of the Oakland Block was remodeled in 1907 to give the building an affluent modern look. The new trend in architecture involved stripping off Victorian ornamentation to make old buildings conform to the latest style. This modern style

marked the beginning of a boring trend in architecture, in my opinion, that has continued up to recent times. With the introduction of steel in building construction, arches were no longer required for structural support in the design. The original arched windows of the Oakland Block, considered to be old-fashioned, were replaced with a symmetrical grid of windows. The remodel also involved lowering the ceiling height of the interior space, as high ceilings and tall windows were no longer needed for light and airflow now that electric fans and light fixtures were available.

The Oakland Block was equipped with the latest mechanical innovations. Besides electricity, a new central steam-heating system was installed in the building. Steam-heat radiators were

The Oakland Block (white building) served as the city hall in the town of Whatcom until the striking red brick Victorian building was constructed in 1903 (now Whatcom Museum).

substituted for the coal-fired, pot-bellied stoves placed every twenty feet (the standard requirement for heating with coal-fired stoves). I might add here that a better way of heating buildings has yet to be invented. Hold onto the steam-heat system if you're lucky enough to find one in your building.

The foundation of the Oakland Block had slipped over the years, making it uneven in many places, and the retail spaces added to the building over time were staggered to match the slope of the land, all of which created thirteen different levels. The top floor of the building

was in terrible condition. After the City Hall moved out of the Oakland building in 1903, this vacant space was converted to serve as one of the better hotels in town. The 20-room hotel was abandoned in the 1970s after a fire gutted the interior. This explained the black boot marks on the doors of the hotel rooms, obviously kicked in by firemen making sure that nobody was trapped inside the burning building.

Despite the condition issues with the Oakland building, its location, size, and historic character gave it great potential. To purchase the property, I was required to pay $190,000 in cash because the owners were convinced that the building was no longer salvageable. They did not want to risk getting it back by carrying a contract to cover any remaining funds. This is when I had my first experience with "hard money lending" and purchase by 1031 exchange, which enabled me to transfer the $100,000 equity from the sale of the Elks Club Building.

In order to get the $90,000 to add to the proceeds from the Elks building, I had to locate a hard moneylender. No one in Bellingham was willing to loan on the building, so I found a lender in Seattle. That money cost me $20,000 or around 20 "points up front." To get the $90K, I also had to pay on a short-term note of $110,000 at a 19% interest rate. Market prices at the time were low, but money was scarce—the direct opposite of the 2008 real estate bubble.

Although the hard money loan to buy the Oakland Block was expensive, I was able to pay it back and get my original $100,000 from the Elks Building sale in a little over a year, because I managed to attract a bank to give me a long-term loan on the building. In effect, I repackaged the building to make it look as if the Oakland Block had a great future and was not a teardown candidate. By changing the bank's perception of the building, I succeeded in getting the loan and saved it from demolition.

To pull off this quick transformation, I repaired the broken windows and fixed the minor repair issues that stood

Stripping away layers to expose the original structure in the second floor of the building.

out from the years of neglect, such as the leaky roof. After making these improvements, the tenants were willing to sign long-term leases for higher rent than the previous owner had been asking.

With the help of my son Tyler, I removed all of the asbestos covering from the pipes in the heating system. The owner is allowed to remove asbestos with proper training. Back in the early 1990s, it was best to learn how to take care of this job yourself, as the expense of hiring professionals to do it could be a real deal breaker. Fortunately, the cost of having asbestos remediation professionally done

An open door at the rear of the Oakland building welcomes new ideas for the restoration.

has come down dramatically in the past 10 years. It is critical to take care of asbestos removal because banks will not put a mortgage on a property that has not been remediated, and all buildings from this time period had asbestos in the original construction in one form or another. This means that your property has to get a clean bill of health from a certified company stating that all toxic material has been removed or is not present. When I was sure that the building was ready for the banks, I brought them in, and because my original investment was so low, I was able to get my money out.

To give this project my full attention, I moved my office and warehouse from the Helena building into the Oakland building and started work on it. First, I cleared out the fire debris and stripped the top two floors down to the studs. I put the

Oakland Block on the National Register and drew out the plans for the "as built," which is a technical term for what a building looks like in the present to compare with the original drawings and assess the best way to renovate the building. Then I began drafting my plans for a prospective renovation.

The triangular structure of this building coupled with the multiple levels made it a real challenge to redesign. It was only by closely studying the building for several years that I was able to think it all out visually and come up with a viable plan. I spent many years working on a plan to convert this building into an apartment complex. Unfortunately, the project proved to be too complex and expensive to do myself in the private sector. The expense was due to the fact that the upper floor of the building had been aban-

Storefront in 2015.

doned after the fire. To get a new occupancy permit, especially for residential occupancy, would require improving everything from upgrading the plumbing and electrical to completing a seismic upgrade for earthquakes, adding a fire suppression system (sprinkler), and providing ADA accessibility for wheel chairs, which usually requires an elevator.

In 2001, I sold the cleaned-up Oakland Block, along with my plans for the remodel and the Historic Registry papers, to the Bellingham Housing Authority for a profit of around $300,000. The Housing Authority went on to build the apartment complex proposed in my plans, and fixed the structural elements of the building. The total cost of that remodel was over $3,500,000. My project budget had to be kept under $1,000,000.

An interesting side note is that the Housing Authority hired its own architectural firm to draw up the plans, and as far as I could tell, they changed little from my original plan. This plan won a national award for Creative Adaptive Reuse of a Historic Property, especially because it did not require the installation of an elevator, as I had created a new entrance on one floor level to supply several accessible units. I was able to come up with this award-winning design because I had worked in the building for over four years and continually improved on the design. It was this design that sold the property.

Daylight Building in 1927, with State Street Garage and Skagg's Safeway Store.
Historic photographs of the Daylight Building courtesy of Whatcom Museum.

Old Buildings Come with a Past:
The Dark Side of the Daylight Building

Daylight Block (1904)
1201-1215 North State Street
Bellingham, Washington

IN A CITY the size of Bellingham, it's possible to find out through the grapevine the owners of the interesting historic downtown properties and the likelihood of their coming up for sale. But I became so busy with my rehab projects that I asked several realtors to be on the lookout for me. I was shocked to see the Daylight Block, one of the major downtown corner properties, pictured on the front cover of the *Bellingham Real Estate Magazine*. I had no idea this building was coming up for sale. The Daylight building was not just a major property, it was the poster boy for the perfect historic fixer upper. This is a building built to last 500 years. It also is a stunning example of the early 20th-century period

View from Chestnut Street north on Elk, Daylight Building at left, 1907.

vernacular. Architect Frank C. Burns designed this building in the Neo-classical style popular in American cities during Bellingham's real estate boom from 1900 to 1915.

From an investment standpoint, the Daylight Block attracted me because of its great integrity. The building had changed very little aesthetically since its construction in 1904, and it had stayed in use as a commercial/residential space since that time. The Daylight Block had been home to many enterprises, including the *Morning Reveille*, Bellingham's oldest newspaper. In addition, the building has a prime location on one of the busiest intersections in town, with 18,000 cars passing the building every day.

I immediately called the phone number on the advertisement to inquire about the property. By that afternoon, I had the building "under contract," which in real estate jargon means that the owner has to sell it to me if I perform everything agreed to in the required time frame. By the terms of the contract, I had only 60 days to put the finance package together.

The kicker was that in order to finance this $600,000 prize building, I would have to come up with over $100,000 cash. My only option was to refinance the Unity Building, which I still owned at the time. No bank, as far as I could ascertain, had loaned money on a downtown building since the mall had opened in 1988. I also needed another loan on the Daylight building; for the remaining $500,000 I had to get two simultaneous loans on two old buildings. Fortunately, a new bank came to town, the Pioneer Bank. Its name proved to be symbolic. As newcomers, they needed to be competitive. The bank was among the first banks in the region to give loans on historic properties.

The two loans from the Pioneer Bank went through exactly on the 60th day. And just in time, because another party made a higher all-cash offer on it the next day. This higher backup offer basically means perform or else you lose. Somehow I could sense that this building and I were meant for each other. I was now the proud owner of the Daylight Block. At last, I felt that I had secured my new profession, for I could see that with the completion of this building, I would no longer need to import sweaters to sustain my renovation business.

From this point forward, I bought or tried to buy every historic property in Bellingham that came up for sale that fit my specifications. Besides the need for a building to be historic and robustly built, and not modified or neglected beyond its potential for restoration, it had to be in use. As long as a building stays in use, the original building codes will be grandfathered into the contract. The other key factor I use to determine the selection of a property is the original price and the projected value after the renovation. The Daylight Block fulfilled every requirement.

Unlike the Oakland Block, the residential portion of the Daylight Building was not abandoned when I purchased the

Byron Grocery Store in the Daylight Building, 1905.

> The Daylight building was named for the many windows and skylights in the architecture. Up until the 1920s, buildings featured large windows on all sides... along with skylights and window wells to allow light into the core of the building.

building. It was still in use, though only marginally. This 36,000-sq.-ft. structure was originally designed with retail space for two 7,000-sq.-ft. retail stores, perhaps the largest stores in town at the time. The second story of the building originally had 40 offices. After the First World War, this space was converted into 28 apartments with four shared bathrooms on the top floor. When I acquired the building, there were tenants living or doing business on all three floors, generating a low rental income. This low income was desirable from an investment standpoint, since a building can only appraise for as high a figure as the recent and present financial history would support (see the chapter on finance in Part Two).

The Daylight Block was solidly built, and still intact, thanks to the fact that its architecture predates the time when electricity became widely used. Buildings up to this "pre-electric" point in time had to be designed so that gas lighting wasn't needed in the daytime. The Daylight building was named for the many windows and skylights in the architecture. Up until the 1920s, buildings featured large windows on all sides, when possible, along with skylights and window wells to allow light into the core of the building. To support these penetrations, the wood framing of the Daylight building was exceptionally strong. In fact, I try to make sure that all of my buildings are built to this standard.

The Daylight Building was without question a significant find. But what a mess. Every room in the building, every corner, and every closet from the basement to the top floor space was crammed full of things. The previous owner, who had recently passed away, was an eccentric collector of a wild assortment of objects. George had inherited the building when it was still functioning as a furniture store and ran it into the ground. At some point, he locked the front door, taped newspaper over the windows, and starting living in the various bedrooms and living rooms that had been set up to showcase furniture.

Because the Daylight Block retail spaces were remodeled in the 1930s to serve as a furniture show room, there were no hallways. Instead, dozens of bookshelves filled with thousands of books were used to partition the space. With no windows and no hallways, it was easy to get lost in the expansive maze of over 15,000 sq. ft. of space on three different levels—and this was only the owner's personal space. There were 15 living

rooms, for each of which he created a special theme. One of the
living rooms displayed only cuff
links—over 1,500 pairs. Another
room displayed seashells—not or-
dinary seashells, but collectable
oddities such as a left-handed
Welch conch shell. It was all, in a
word, *overwhelming*.

Cleared of debris, the massive 12,000 sq. ft. basement is ready for transformation.

The basement space of the
building was set up to manufac-
ture furniture. There was a huge
woodworking tool from the 1920s
featuring a band saw with an
18-foot blade. The wood planer weighed
over 500 pounds. There also was a mat-
tress-stuffing machine, and truckloads
of bolts of material for upholstering furniture (which, although exotic and rare,
proved to be worthless because of its condition). In one section of the basement,
there were perhaps a hundred pieces of
furniture, from some long-lost era, in various states of construction.

To give you a sense of the size of the
owner's collection, we discovered a car
buried underneath the piles of stuff in the
basement—a 1959 Ford Edsel with only
29,000 miles on it. Apparently, George
had permanently parked the car there
with gas still in the tank when he moved
into the building.

Because of the reputation of its eccentric owner, the Daylight Block was considered to be very odd as well. I learned
more than I probably cared to know about
George when the building came into my

hands. Not only did I inherit a lot of his
personal records, including his travel
journals and photo albums, but I also
learned about this odd character from
the stories everybody told me about him.
George was 6' 7" tall and rather portly. He
had the habit of dressing in a top hat and
tails and strutting around the downtown.

During the day, he taught Russian
egg-painting classes to old ladies at the
Whatcom County Museum. At night, he
filmed dirty movies in which he starred
as the main character. The videocassettes
he left behind were enough to fill a two-
yard dumpster.

I could go on to tell more stories about
George's personal life, as I became inti-
mately connected with this character in
the process of sorting through his possessions, one piece at a time. Stories also cir-
culated in the community because of the
kind of tenants he attracted to the building. One of the remaining retail tenants

The addition of a decorative cornice with a fanlight motif to match the clearstory.

(at the time I purchased the building) was the owner of a porn shop with private video booths. Only seven of the 28 upstairs rooms were rented, and two of those tenants were drug dealers who sold marijuana out of their second-story windows by conveying it in buckets on strings down to the street.

George originally intended to give the Daylight Block and all of his possessions to the Bellingham Theater Guild, as he was one of its early founders. That explains the huge collection of theatrical props and costumes we found stored in the building, with sections for Christmas and Easter and clothes from various time periods. By an interesting twist of fate, not long before his death, George reconnected with his only child, a young man of 20 who had been raised in Norway by George's former wife. The young man wanted to meet his father, whom he had not seen since his mother left the country with him as a baby. George was so taken by his son that he changed his will and bequeathed his entire estate to him. Shortly, George suffered an aneurism and died.

The son and his wife came back to Bellingham and put the Daylight Block up for sale. To rid themselves of the contents of the building, they organized several auctions. Needless to say, they were overwhelmed by the amount of stuff accumulated in George's massive collection, including over 37,000 books. I know this number, as book dealers from all over the state came to bid on the books, which were sold in bulk at public auctions. We reached an agreement whereby I would dispose of everything that didn't sell at auction, except for any remaining books and two items that I wanted to purchase myself: the Edsel and a Polynesian outrigger canoe that originally hung over the bar at Trader Vic's in Seattle. At it turned out, the owners generated more money from the auctions than they received from the sale of their building.

The refurbishing of the Daylight Block took more than twelve years to complete. We tackled several larger projects over the years on the building, but never at the same time. I want to point out, once again, that for a building of this size, it's best to spread out the remodel over time so as not to trigger the need to hire an architect or engineer except in very specific defined spaces. I also needed to refinance the property several times to get the capitol to complete the renovation.

Restoring the original brick façade.

The work that the previous owner had completed on the building was limited to quick patchwork. George, unfortunately, like many owners of old buildings, was running the property as if it would ultimately be torn down. Whereas I treated the building as if it would be around for another 500 years—which I believe it will.

We started the renovation with the 12,000-sq.-ft. daylight basement. To finance the replacement of the windows and doors, I received a federal community development loan through the City Planning Department. The basement had once served as a parking garage with access to the street, making it easy to renovate the space. We blazed a road through the basement as we sorted through the piles of stored material, and eventually made our way to the exit on the far side. After a year of constant work, the stuff was either sold or hauled to the dump. Ironically, my first tenant in the basement was the owner of a secondhand store who rented the space for the next five years.

Once it was filled with racks of clothing and assorted items, the basement looked almost the same as it had before.

In the second phase of the project, we focused on cleaning up the ten vacant residential units that surrounded the large window well on the second floor. The units had been abandoned and condemned by

The exposed brick wall and refurbished hardwood floor add warmth and historic character to the apartment.

order of the fire department as a result of a fire in the Alaska Block, a similar building on the same street, just around the corner. The Alaska Block was also designed by Frank Burns and constructed in the same year as the Daylight Block. Several people had been killed in that fire because there was only one fire exit in the building. With the help of the fire marshal, I was able to resolve this egress issue by putting an interior stairwell out of the window well and onto the fire escape. This upgrade increased the revenue of the building by $2,500 a month. We went through all ten rooms, one by one, and brought them up to decent standards.

After about five years, I had full occupancy of the residential units, which increased the value of the building based on this new "stabilized" value. With the proceeds from a refinance based on those figures, I was able to make two large capital improvements. We put a sprinkler system in the basement to meet code regulations so the space could be rented out as an assembly area for a nightclub. We

put scaffolding around the exterior of the building and replaced the cornice at the top, installed awnings on the front of the building, and repaired parts of the façade damaged by tree growth between the bricks and mortar. This was also a good time to repair and repaint the windows. These upgrades cost around $150,000, but were worth the investment. They transformed the Daylight Block from a rundown, derelict building into a dignified presence on the street.

With this new look, the quality of the tenants we attracted improved, and the rent income generated improved as well because of the upgrades. The income of this property increased from the original $6,000 per month to $36,000 per month as of now, and the value of the building increased from $600,000 to over $4,500,000. Note that the value is well over 100 times the monthly rent (see the finance chapter for details on this magic math formula). The Daylight Block has been refinanced many times in order to invest in other commercial properties, including the two historic buildings we owned directly across the street: the twin hotels, the Laube and the Windsor, constructed in the same year as the Daylight Block. If you plan to make a major improvement to a building, it is best to own the surrounding properties whenever possible. Not only will you avoid the risk of having an owner of an adjoining property whose poor management could bring down the neighborhood, but your investment will also increase the value of the entire block.

In this chapter, I have gone into the ownership background of the Daylight Block to give readers the feeling of what it's like to work with the history of these properties. Buying an old building means more than dealing with the physical problems associated with transforming a building from an eyesore in the community to the pride of the city. It gets you

involved in the lives, and sometimes the psychology, of the people who originally owned the building. I have found that it takes around ten years for a property with a good name to go bad, and about half that time to get rid of the bad name and negative associations after the renovation has been completed. The Daylight Block today is leased to capacity and home to the largest nightclub in the county. The Daylight is an example of the perfect investment property. You could invest in just one property comparable in size and quality to the Daylight, and live very comfortably on your building's income stream.

The main section of the Daylight basement, converted into a nightclub.

View of downtown Bellingham from Sehome Hill in 1929. The Hotel Leopold (right of center) was a popular destination for motor tourists. Photograph courtesy of Whatcom Museum.

Facing page: Morse Hardware Company celebrated its 75th anniversary in the Leopold Hotel's Crystal Ballroom in 1959. Photograph courtesy of Whatcom Museum.

The Golden Age of the Grand Hotel

Leopold Building/Hotel (1899, 1910)
1224 Cornwall Avenue
Bellingham, Washington

IN ITS HEYDAY during the early 20th century, the Hotel Leopold in the heart of downtown Bellingham was the premier hotel in northern Washington. This elegant and imposing hotel, rising ten stories high, was once a popular gathering place for the rich and famous. Its guests included U.S. Presidents, European royalty, and Hollywood celebrities. The hotel also played an important role as a vibrant social center for the community.

With the construction of the ten-story Leopold tower in 1929, the hotel occupancy increased to 500 rooms. Photograph courtesy of Whatcom Museum.

Every major American city in existence before 1940 had at least one of these landmark hotels where the public held festive events. Hotels of the quality of the Leopold rarely come on the market, and I was excited when it became available in 2005. The Leopold building is, in my estimation, one of the top five architectural gems in the city.

The original building at this location was the Byron Hotel, constructed by Captain H.C. Byron in 1899, during a dramatic growth period when it was speculated that Bellingham would become the terminus of the Great Northern Railroad. The Byron Hotel changed ownership (and eventually names) in 1910 when Leopold Schmidt, brew master and founder of the Bellingham Bay Brewery, bought the hotel. The brown brick hotel structure was designed in the Chicago style with Mission influences, such as the red roof tile and round arches, and the decorative Spanish tile of the hotel façade and interior.

The Leopold Building, 2015.

Photographer: David H. Johnston

Over the years, the original hotel was modified to adapt to the times. The 1913 hotel, which consisted of 200 rooms, later expanded with two new additions. The Tulip room, known today as the Crystal Ballroom, was added in 1922. In 1929, the Leopold tower was added, a ten-story structure that increased the hotel's number of rooms to 500. Grand hotels like the Leopold couldn't compete with the inexpensive motels that sprang up in the 1950s and '60s. To keep pace with the times, the owner demolished part of the building in 1967 to make room for a parking structure and a motel-style addition with an outdoor swimming pool.

The Leopold hotel changed identity again in the 1980s, when it was converted from a full-service hotel into a retirement living community. The developers were a large company that owned and operated retirement centers. The building underwent major renovations to convert the hotel for residential use. This involved combining the hotel rooms into decent sized units and equipping each of them with a kitchen, which is essential for renting units as residential space. This conversion was a major selling point to myself and my two partners, David Johnston and my son Kane Hall, as the cost of converting these old hotels into residential space is tremendous.

What these grand old hotels have going for them, from an investment standpoint, is their central downtown location, which gives them bonus potential for revitalizing the downtown, and a multitude of rooms with potential for conversion to residential use. The Leopold had both a vibrant downtown location and residential units leased almost to capacity. The mechanical side of the building, on the other hand, needed a lot of work. There also was a catch to buying the Leopold building. To purchase this property, my partners and I had to buy the existing retirement business. This went against one of my cardinal rules: "No retail."

If you buy an old hotel building, you may feel a temptation to take over an existing business in the building, such as a shop, a restaurant, or a bar. Often times a tenant will decide to leave, and you, as the new owner and landlord, will inherit whatever they leave behind—including all the equipment you would need to run the business. After a few failed attempts at taking over a former business, I vowed to stay focused on my core business of being a landlord. In the case of the Leopold, however, if we wanted to buy the building, we had no choice but to assume ownership of the Leopold Retirement Residence. Fortunately, the center was well planned and well run when we inherited it, and it continues to attract seniors because of its central location and historic architecture.

The previous owners of the Leopold failed, in my view, to appreciate the reason that retired people would choose to take up residence in this unique building: *nostalgia*. People enjoy the romantic afterglow of the hotel's historic past, a time

Today the Leopold serves as an elegant retirement residence.

when its glamorous hotel ballrooms and restaurants were in full swing. During the renovation of the hotel, the previous owners managed to uncover its distinctive original architecture. They brought back the Mission character of the ground floor space by refurbishing the decorative Spanish tile in the foyer and lobby, and replaced historic details, such as the original lion's head spout in the fountain of the main lobby and the gigantic crystal ball in the ballroom. But much of the original character was removed or dumbed down to fit the previous owner's mold for a retirement center.

We have done our best to open the architecture of the Leopold back up to restore the integrity of this magnificent heritage building. The 5,000 sq. ft. ballroom is now refitted with its original spinning disco ball and new formal drapery in the windows. The ballroom has been reopened to the community for special events such as weddings and civic events—just like in the old days. This one change has put the spice back into the hotel, and it gives the residents a sense of living in a special, culturally thriving environment.

The original St. Helens was designed in the Victorian style popular in the late 19th century.
Photographs of the St. Helens courtesy of Lewis County Historic Museum.

Rebuilding an Image: From Public Nuisance to Community Pride

St. Helens Inn (1917-1921)
440 N. Market Boulevard
Chehalis, Washington

THE ST. HELENS INN, located in the small city of Chehalis, Washington, was once the largest hotel between Portland and Tacoma. This triangular-shaped, six-story building has dominated Old Town Chehalis since the architecture was built in 1917 to replace the original three-story wooden hotel structure built in 1894. William Fraser West, son of pioneer developer William West, hired architect Charles E. Troutman to rebuild the hotel in the

ST HELENS HOTEL. — CHEHALIS. WASHINGTON 9A-H868

The St. Helens Inn was a popular tourist destination from the 1920s to the 1950s when Highway 99 routed through downtown Chehalis.

St. Helens Inn, 1960s.

Neoclassical style popular for commercial structures of that period. Two stories were added to the St. Helens in 1920, expanding the total gross size to 70,000 sq. ft. The hotel featured 140 rooms, two restaurants, and a ballroom.

The St. Helens attracted a steady stream of businessmen and well-heeled motor tourists when Highway 99 routed traffic through downtown Chehalis, but with the construction of the interstate freeway system in the late 1950s, the Inn lost its clientele.

When the hotel's popularity declined in the mid-1970s, it went into foreclosure, and the local bank took the building through a full conversion into a 55-room apartment building. Unfortunately, the interior finishes were standard for the time, and when the hotel was converted into modern apartments, all the historic detail of the interior was lost. Still, this impressive glazed terracotta, six-story triangular building, with a 180-foot awning, was a real beauty from the outside. I could see its potential. The building is located only 120 miles south of Bellingham, making it possible for me to hire a local crew and personally direct the renovation.

The prospect for restoring the St. Helens looked bright. However, an old building comes with the image it has acquired in its community. In a town the size of Chehalis, with a population of about 8,000 people, a place like the St. Helens is impossible to ignore. By the time I bought the building, it had become an embarrassment, as it was badly run-down and under poor management. The St. Helens had such a bad reputation that it would take some effort to turn that image around.

St. Helens Inn, 2014.

When I bought the property, the Chief of Police, whose office was across the street, said to me: "You didn't buy *in* the wrong part of town, you bought *the* wrong part of town."

My project partner and I soon learned the truth of that remark. When we checked the police report for the St. Helens address, we found many mentions of the police being called there. In fact, it was the number one address on the police blotter. This was because the previous owner leased to anybody who could come up with a non-refundable damage deposit of $200 and the first month's rent; he never required credit or criminal reports. In previous years, the city had closed down the residential floors of the building at various times for health violations. On one occasion, the owner paraded the evicted

St. Helens symbol in tilework.

tenants around the building as a publicity stunt to get back at the city officials. That incident gave the building a lot of negative attention.

I wasn't too disturbed by this history, as the replacement cost for a building of this size and character would be around $7,000,0000. I viewed the St. Helens as a large Daylight Building that through persistence would pay off down the road, not only for me, but the community as well. The price was around $1,500,000, which is approximately $25 per sq. ft. New construction for a building like this would now be around $200 per sq. ft. What this building also had going for it, besides its size and great purchase price, was modern mechanical systems—the two biggies being plumbing and electrical, and a solid structure.

The ballroom of the St. Helens and one of the adjoining restaurants had operated as a gambling casino, until smoking was banned from public space and the casino shut down. The other restaurant space in the building was in use as a Lighthouse Mission when we purchased the property. We found a new and better home for the Mission, as this type of service is a bad fit for a large residential apartment. The other tenants on the ground floor included an evangelical church, which proved too noisy for that location, a tax consultant— and to round it out, a palm reader.

Few permits were required to complete the renovation, since the upgrades on the St. Helens mainly involved new finishes, carpets, and appliances. I had at least two men working continually on the project for the five years it took to complete the work. I would never rent out a unit that I would not feel comfortable living in myself. This is the standard I used to rehab the apartments in the St Helens. We went through the units one by one, as tenants were either evicted or moved out, averaging about one or two units a month, at a cost of around $5,000 per unit. The units were given new appliances, carpets, drapes, baseboard electric heaters, and new toilets, and the wood window frames were rebuilt and refurbished.

The one place in the building where I splurged was on the ground floor. I knew that if I wanted the people living upstairs in the old hotel to feel special, as the tenants did in the past when the hotel was first converted to an apartment complex, I would have to invest some time and money in converting the retail shops back to their original condition.

This conversion was handled the same way as my previous projects. We started by tearing out the hung ceiling to access the overhead lighting from the clearstory, and put in newer heating systems. I also knew that it would be important to attract some type of restaurant that was not primarily a bar. I have found

My rule of thumb for buying an old building is that the original timber-frame and masonry core of the architecture must be structurally sound.

that tenants prefer to live and work above a restaurant or a coffee shop, not above a bar. I spent well over my budget to attract this desirable tenant by building out new ADA bathrooms and giving the new tenant a generous Tenant Improvement Allowance, so that the space would work for their business. Now, in place of the casino, there is a large popular bakery in the building. The building is, in a sense, a big house, and every house should have a kitchen, the bigger, the better.

With this project, I think we succeeded in giving the St. Helens Inn a new lease on life. Once again, the community views this iconic building with pride.

Downtown Spokane in 1908, Peyton Building on the right. Photograph courtesy of the Northwest Museum of Arts and Culture.

Facing page: The Peyton Building/Peyton Annex, 2015.

Every Big Town Needs a "Million Dollar Corner"

Peyton Building/Peyton Annex
(1889, 1908)
722 W. Sprague Ave./10 N. Post St.
Spokane, Washington

THE PEYTON BUILDING/Peyton Annex in Spokane, Washington, is the largest commercial building that I own, standing seven stories high, with a gross square footage of over 120,000 sq. ft. The architecture of this property is exquisite, and a great example of the quality detailing and craftsmanship of the

Photographer: David H. Johnston

Photographs courtesy of the Northwest Museum of Arts and Culture.

The Great Eastern Building in 1898 after the Great Fire that devastated Spokane.

commercial structures built in Spokane during the Arts and Crafts movement.

The Spokane area experienced rapid growth after the Northern Pacific Railway was constructed in 1881, making Spokane the transportation hub for the Inland Northwest Empire. New wealth from the mining and timber industries made it one of the most prosperous cities in the state of Washington. Spokane's architectural heritage from that boom time is superb. There was a large inventory of old classic buildings of all sizes on the market in the 1990's when I was on the lookout for more investment property. The Peyton Building had served as the headquarters

for the Spokane Stock Exchange from 1897-1991, which was founded mainly to trade stock in mining companies.

The earlier history of the Peyton Building is worth mentioning. The Peyton rose from the ashes of the Great Eastern Building that burned down in the fire that destroyed most of downtown Spokane in 1889. Colonel Isaac N. Peyton purchased the Great Eastern property and its ruins, and built the Peyton with the salvaged exterior walls of the burned building. Architects Cutter & Malmgren designed the new building, retaining the façade features of the Great Eastern. The Colonel expanded the building in 1908 by

Peyton Building in 1935. Photograph courtesy of the Northwest Museum of Arts and Culture.

attaching the seven-story Peyton Annex, designed by architect Robert Sweatt. The Peyton Building and Annex stand together as one of the largest commercial structures designed in the Commercial and Romanesque revival styles in downtown Spokane.

Although the Peyton Annex has seen extensive alterations over the years, the architecture retains a high level of integrity. In one wing of the Peyton Annex, all of the woodwork, from the doors—well over a hundred—to the windows and floor trim, is sheathed in copper as a fire protection. The exterior storefronts of the Annex are faced with unglazed terra cotta pilasters with egg and dart molding. The exquisite architecture is a testament to the prosperity of the patrons who frequented the retail stores and professional offices of the building. At the time of its construction, the prime commercial location of the Peyton building was referred to as the "million-dollar corner." The ground floor of the building provided some of Spokane's most desired retail space. Many businesses have enjoyed long-standing success on this highly trafficked corner.

When I bought the Peyton Building, it was undergoing a major rehab estimated to cost over $4,000,000. Since this rehab was not complete, we made sure that the building was appraised for the value "as if" it was completed. By doing this, more than $500,000 was kept in a reserve account to be used to complete the renovations. If we had not appraised the building at as if value, we would have been required to do the work with our own cash or secure a construction loan. Fortunately, in this case, the building was so close to completion that the bank was inclined to agree to our terms.

The Peyton Building purchase enabled me to expand my company's investment portfolio at a time when I did not want to be limited to working in Bellingham alone. It's wise not to put all your eggs in one basket in this line of work, especially when you want to look good to a bank or outside investor. The bank will want to see that you're broad based and not privy to the economy of any one town. Purchasing this building gave me the opportunity to own a large historic commercial property, as the few buildings of this size in Bellingham rarely come up for sale. My knowledge of commercial real estate expanded greatly by owning a legacy property of this scale, and in a large town with a rich architectural heritage.

The Romanesque Revival style of the Peyton Annex contrasts with the Peyton Building's red brick Commercial style.

Herald Building, under construction, 1926. The advent of steel and reinforced concrete modernized commercial building style. Photos by J.W. Sandison, author's collection.

Built for the Future:
The Legacy of Old Buildings

Bellingham Herald Building
1155 N. State Street
Bellingham, Washington

THE BELLINGHAM HERALD BUILDING commands the downtown block of North State Street in the business district above Bellingham Bay. This striking white building rises seven stories high from the front, or nine stories from the alley, counting the mezzanine level on the ground floor and the penthouse suite on the roof level. The 40-foot "Herald" sign on the roof is a prominent landmark in the city. Architect Frederick Stanley Piper, with Seattle architects Morrison and Stimson, designed the distinctive Late Gothic Revival architecture. To construct this massive building, the architects incorporated

The Herald Building in the 1920s. Courtesy of Whatcom Museum.

"Hooray for the Herald." School children get a tour of the new Herald Building in 1926.
Photo by J.W. Sandison, courtesy of Whatcom Museum.

Rolling newspapers for delivery in the basement of the Herald Building, 1926. Photo by J.W. Sandison, courtesy of
Whatcom Museum.

The Herald Building showcases elements of the ornate Gothic style in the elegant archway of its front entrance.

fabricated steel and reinforced concrete, which started to be widely used for commercial buildings in the 1920s.

The Bellingham Herald Building was constructed in 1926 for the Bellingham Publishing Company. The building originally housed a newspaper plant for Bellingham's morning newspaper, the *Morning Reveille*, as well as the evening paper, the *Bellingham Herald*, until the *Reveille* was discontinued in 1927. The *Bellingham Herald* (for which the building was renamed) is the most widely read newspaper in Whatcom County. The architect's original floor plan included 140 offices, accessed by twin elevators, with the newspapers housed on the first floor and office space on the upper floors. In addition to the newspaper's offices, the Herald Building housed medical practices, retail, and other professional businesses.

Landmark buildings of the quality of the Herald Building don't often come up for sale. The Herald Building fits the Criterion A classification of the National Register of Historic Places for its iconic architecture and historic significance. It also is designated as a Class A office building in real estate terms: the highest quality building in its market, well built with high quality infrastructure, well-located, with plenty of on-site parking, and a lot of empty offices. The Herald Building's close proximity to our other properties on North State Street, the Daylight Building and the twin hotels, the Laube and the Windsor, made the Herald an ideal prospect.

The Herald Building came on the market in fall 2008 at the height of the recession. The asking price was only $30 per sq. foot. So the potential for this investment was excellent. However, banks were not eager to loan money on commercial properties, especially not a property forced to go on the market in a fire sale. The parent company owning the *Bellingham Herald*, and accounting for over 70% of the rent (as they leased over

Tearing out the hung ceiling restores the original proportions of the design.

The old vault is refurbished.

38,000 sq. ft.), was on the verge of bank-ruptcy. We had to come up with cash. The transaction involved a hard money loan from a private party, but the deal went down after six months of negotiating. The funds generated from a reappraisal of the St. Helens Inn were used to finance the first phase of the ground floor renovation in the Herald Building—although it took five years to renovate and rent the St. Helens before we could secure the loan.

The Herald Building is the largest single project I have worked on during my career. The building had been remod-eled in 1980 to reconfigure the space. The rehab included the removal of some walls in the basement and first floor, as well as modifications to the basement restrooms.

On the exterior of the building, the alter-ations had included reconfiguring doors on the alley and re-glazing windows. Over the years, some of the original mahogany doors and transoms had been replaced. Dropped ceilings and contemporary fluor-escent light were added on all floors. Wood paneling covered up the brass trim and pressed tin ceiling of the elevators.

Our plan for the renovation involved restoring the six retail spaces on the ground level and bringing back the orig-inal window bays and mezzanine space of each unit. We didn't start working on the first three floors of the building right away because the *Bellingham Herald* was still operating in that space when we pur-chased the building. In 2012, the newspa-

The ground floor is gutted to the supporting pillars to reconfigure the space as originally designed. The original terrazzo flooring is salvaged.

per moved out of its 15,000 sq. ft. main floor location, and part of the basement, into its present 8,000 sq. ft. space on the second floor. Then we were able to move forward with the renovation. Our goal was to restore the six separate retail spaces of the original design when the building was constructed.

The building's concrete and steel construction made it possible to entirely gut out the ground floor to the supporting pillars and reconfigure the space as originally designed by the architect. At first, I went back and forth as to whether or not to do the entire ground floor, as the two larger spaces were rentable as they were. But I've learned that once you start a remodel and fix the worst part of a building or space, other parts that seemed acceptable at first, now look bad by comparison and bring down the entire project. So I decided to rehab the entire ground floor

Steel studs are used to bring the floor plan back to what it was in 1926.

The old printing press room on State Street is ready for conversion to retail space.

The old web press room, looking east, during renovation.

After the rehab—the old brick wall, ceiling and mezzanine are restored to life as the Rock and Rye Oyster Bar.

at the same time. As with our previous renovations, the rehab crew went through the rest of the building, one floor/office at a time. We applied new paint and flooring, salvaging as much of the original wood and terrazzo flooring as possible. We tore out the hung ceilings along the way. Even though tearing out the ceiling only gained us about 18 inches of height, this added height is important if you want to expose the original ceiling and re-establish the original proportions of the rooms. Some of the original wooden windows had to be rebuilt, especially those facing south, but the rest of them only needed repainting. The re-introduction of the renovated Herald Building back into the community made a very dramatic change and was well received.

As in the case of the St. Helens building, the renovation of the Herald Building's ground floor retail space has attracted excellent retail and restaurant tenants. Our first tenant was the owner of a glamorous oyster bar that opened in 2014. Western Washington University signed a lease in that same year to open offices in our prominent corner street-level space.

The Herald Building is an important addition to our company's portfolio of properties. The revenue generated from renting the available space in this building enables us to launch new projects and maintain our existing properties. The new bank appraisal we received after completing the first $1 million renovation of the Herald Building valued the

View of the Herald building from the alley.

property at $10 million. With the loan proceeds, we moved forward with the full-scale renovation of the Herald Building and purchased more properties in downtown Bellingham.

These days, I prefer to play a managerial role overseeing our buildings, rather than focus my attention on acquiring more property. But I do make exceptions. I will continue to buy old buildings in the downtown that call me to their rescue. And I will buy eyesores that have no historic value but are strategically located in relation to my other buildings. Cleaning up those buildings helps to revitalize the historic character of the downtown as well.

With the renovation of the Herald Building, I think it is safe to say that the future of Bellingham's historic heritage in the downtown business district is assured.

Facing page: Bellingham Hardware, courtesy of Whatcom Museum.

PART TWO

The Nuts 'n Bolts of the Old Building Business

Railroad Avenue, 1905. Photograph courtesy of Whatcom Museum.

Tips and Guidelines for Doing It Yourself

MANY OF THE OLD BUILDINGS in our cities and towns are being treated like an old horse from back in the days before the invention of the motorcar. The owner is just trying to get one more day's work out of the beast before it collapses. If the building is going to be torn down anyway, why put money into it, especially a costly upgrade such as a new roof? Because of this attitude, the repairs that you'll find in old commercial buildings are often slapdash and cosmetic. In some cases, the basic structure of the building will be too far gone to make it a candidate for restoration. But often times, you will find a great enduring spirit buried underneath the surface. When you consider that these buildings were originally built to last for centuries, a hundred-year-old building should have a good long life ahead of it.

There still are plenty of viable old buildings just waiting for the right owner to rescue them. Unfortunately, often because of their surface appearance and intimidating scale, many urban developers think that tearing them down and building new is the only way to be successful. I hope to turn that attitude around by showing the enormous potential in the old building market, and the surprising ease with which many old buildings can be restored to a fully healthy life.

Investing in distressed urban buildings has proved very profitable for me over the years. And it is rewarding beyond words to see a failing downtown business district being transformed back into a vibrant place with true character. Even renovating only one of these historic buildings will have an impact on revitalizing your downtown.

Part Two is essentially a do-it-yourself guide for handling the basics of the historic restoration business. I will show you how to find and purchase property that is ripe for redevelopment, introduce you to a system for rehabbing your building to bring it back into full public use, and give you practical guidelines for leasing and managing your property. Most important, you will learn how to make your building pay for the cost of the rehab and give you a profit into the future. Investing in old buildings is like playing leapfrog. When one building is completed, it provides the money through a refinance to buy and fix up the next one.

It takes commitment to hold your vision through to the end on a restoration that takes years to complete. But it's well worth the effort. With careful planning, hands-on resourcefulness, and hopefully, a passion for saving old buildings, you'll enjoy the journey.

Photograph courtesy of Whatcom Museum.

How to Find and Purchase
an Old Building

Photographer: Jason Koski

Photographer: Jason Koski

When a Building Calls You

WHENEVER I FIND a good quality historic building for sale, I often think of it like an adoption. Sometimes I can feel the building call out to me to take it back to its original glory, almost like an orphan abandoned on the street. If you decide to purchase an old building yourself, it's important to feel a connection with it, since this property will take up your time and energy for years to come. So finding one that attracts you enough to want to buy it is the place to start. You can often tell from a building's exterior appearance what kind of life it has experienced, and whether or not it's likely to be a good rehab candidate. But to be sure about a building's potential, you'll have to do some research. Not all old historic properties—no matter how attractive—are viable for redevelopment. Before taking on the ownership of an old building, make sure to look into every aspect of the building's history and condition.

In this chapter, I will show you what makes a historic building worth buying and guide you through the steps for purchasing a property, from completing the research to signing the deed. It's important to be well prepared when you purchase an old building for the first time.

#1 Goal: Find a Building Worth Your Investment

It is vital that the building you're thinking of buying will prove to be a good investment property. You don't want to get saddled with a property that can't be turned around to make a decent profit. The stories earlier in the book illustrate unfortunate cases where the owners (myself included) were forced to sell their property because they got stuck in the middle of what proved to be a difficult rehab. To avoid that situation, use the guidelines below to determine an old building's viability. If the building in question doesn't meet these standards, it probably would not be worth your investment.

What to Look for When Buying an Old Building

Historic Character and Built to Last

- Look for a solidly built structure that's constructed with durable quality materials. This almost always means a building with a thick masonry exterior of brick or stone, and heavy timber framing on the interior.
- A fully operational building with only the finishes damaged can greatly reduce the purchase price. However, make sure that these damages will not exceed the building's potential for restoration. Damages beyond viable restoration would include irreparable alteration of the exterior masonry or the interior wood frame.
- Superficial cosmetic damage is easy to clean up and refurbish. For example, look for a remodeled or modernized façade; chances are, the original front of the building is hidden underneath. The same might be true for the ceilings and interior walls, as it easier to apply the new over the old than to rip out the original surfaces. This can serve as a model for restoring the remainder of the building.
- Every building requires routine upgrades for mechanical and electrical systems, and old buildings are no exception. Since older buildings often experience neglect, expect to eventually upgrade a building's systems.
- Watch out for deal breakers that would require doing more than repair, such as having to immediately replace the sewer and water system or the entire electrical system. Check to see if the roof, plumbing, or sewer has been leaking for many years, in which case, the entire structure might not be salvageable due to the damaged wood and/or mold issues. These issues are typically found in abandoned buildings that have not been in use for years.

Original Architecture of the Building Is Intact

- If the original structural design of a building has been significantly modified, that will make the rehab difficult and even cost prohibitive. These modifications were usually done as modernizations to the front of the building; in such cases, often the entire façade was removed or significantly altered.
- For historic buildings without significant alterations, investors have access to generous tax incentives. Every building over 50 years old is historic by definition. The National Register of Historic Places (NRHP)

offers a 20% tax credit on qualifying historic buildings, or a 10% tax credit on historic buildings over 50 years old but not on the registry. Historic and non-historic criteria differ significantly,[1] with simplicity favoring non-historic buildings. In essence, any major alteration to a historic building will disqualify it from nomination as a candidate for the National Register. However, even without NRHP registration, a building may still receive non-historic benefits if it meets the following criteria:

- 50% of external walls must remain as external walls;
- 75% of walls must remain as internal or external walls;
- 75% of internal framework must remain unaltered;
- The building will not be converted to residential.

Currently in Use

Look for buildings that have been abused and neglected, but are not entirely abandoned. If the building is still in use, it is far easier to restore it back to life.

- **Building codes.** As long as a building stays in use, even marginal current use, the original building codes will be grandfathered into the contract. If the building has been vacant for over one year, however, the local building department may tell you, "Grandpa is dead." So look for a building that is in use. If the building has not been in permanent use since it was first built, it might need to be brought up to modern standards before you can receive a new occupancy permit. For example, bringing your building up to code might require the installation of a fire suppression system (sprinkled), seismic upgrades, an elevator—or perhaps all three.
- **The Profit and Loss Statement.** Another important reason to purchase an occupied building is that it will affect the property value reported on your Profit and Loss (P & L) statement. In effect, the value of the building is based upon the value of the underlying land and its income or rent. When you bring the vacant units back into use, the rent increases the value as if it was built from scratch. For example, if only one of five units in an apartment building is rentable, then the value of

---

1   NRHP tax credit information for historical/non-historical buildings: http://www.nps.gov/tps/tax-incentives.htm

the four empty units would be zero dollars. The P & L is based on the property's monthly income and expenses.

You can use the P & L statement to get an appraisal of the property and secure a first mortgage from a bank. The illustration below shows a common P & L statement used to appraise a property. The statement considers an entire year's worth of income and expenses. For easy book keeping, accountants assign numbers to each account based on a predetermined list known as the "chart of accounts." As you might imagine, each number to the left of an account name represents the account's number. Simply put, each account that generates money is placed at the top, with expense accounts in the middle, and all the money left over at the bottom. P & L statements also help the investor make decisions by showing which areas (expenses) of the building could be improved for greater profitability, and which areas (income) should be generating more money.

On the other hand, if the building is vacant, then it's highly unlikely that you'll be able to secure a first mortgage, because the building will have no income stream to support a loan payment. Unless the loan is connected to a construction loan.[2] With a construction loan, an appraisal can be projected for the value of the building after the renovation is completed. Securing a construction loan is far more difficult, as banks want to see a proven history of completed projects done by you before they will risk their money.

Company Name
Building Name
January through December 2014

INCOME

4000 - Revenue

4100 - Revenue - Commercial Rent	81,734.64
4200 - Revenue - Residential Rent	56,227.10
4240 - Triple-Net-Income	6,243.36
4250 - Late Fees	1,310.00
4270 - Laundry Income	1,212.00
Total Income	**146,727.10**

EXPENSE

5540 - Repairs & Maintenance	8,299.35
5570 - Advertising	20.00
5680 - Janitor Cleaning Labor	8,534.41
5681 - Janitorial Supplies	799.52
5710 - Management Fees	10,986.47
5717 - Insurance	1,670.50
5720 - Monitoring and Inspections	734.00
5315 - Mortgage Interest	37,056.37
5740 - Utility - Electric	2,436.63
5745 - Utility - Gas	3,176.00
5760 - Utility - Garbage	1,457.50
5780 - Utility - Water and Sewer	4,304.92
5790 - Taxes Expense	21.59
5860 - Property Taxes	8,202.35
Total Expense	**87,699.61**
NET INCOME	**59,027.49**

---

2   A bank loan tailored towards the needs of a builder. Loan term is typically less than one year, with the borrower only paying interest while construction takes place.

Another option would be for the owner to carry a private contract.[3] However, this rarely happens, as the seller must own the building "free and clear" to carry a first mortgage. The only option for buying a property with no tenants (abandoned) would be to pay all cash. Many times, the owners of such properties are willing to sell for only the land value less the tear down cost, in which case the building comes with the land for free.

Good Location

There are plenty of old buildings with great historic character that unfortunately would not be worth the investment because of their location.

- Avoid buying a building in a seriously blighted or unsafe neighborhood or in an area not easily accessed due to urban development (e.g., new construction, highways).
- Look for an attractive building in a prime location in terms of transportation and accessibility. This will make an enormous difference in both the short- and long-term success of your project.
- Buy a building that you could envision living in or having a business in yourself.
- Buy on the corner if possible. Corners are the prominent building sites and usually have the biggest and best buildings; hence, they are the key properties to develop first in the old downtowns. When the corner buildings are restored and anchored with happy tenants, redevelopment of the middle of the block will follow.

Good Projected Value After Renovation

When you calculate the cost of your prospective renovation compared to its purchase price, make sure that you come out ahead (see "magic math formula" in the next chapter). Simply check that the increase in rent from renovation will cover the monthly payment on the loan used to finance the construction.

---

3   A financing arrangement between a building's current owner and the buyer. For example, the buyer uses the building while making regular monthly payments to the owner for 5 years. Then, the buyer takes the 5-year track record to a bank to qualify for a loan that pays the remaining loan balance with the owner. After paying the owner with the loan, the buyer fully owns the building and makes regular payments to a bank.

Initial Steps Before Purchase

Your Due Diligence

We will talk in detail in the finance chapter about getting a property under contract, which means that you and the seller have agreed to certain terms while you proceed with your due diligence, and the seller is committed to sell the property to you for those agreed terms provided you do not change your offer while you investigate the property. Here I will walk you through the basics. The 30-day "due diligence" period on your contract gives you time to fully research a property before you pay the bank for an appraisal. Make sure to complete a careful background check and inspection of the property. Schedule a meeting with your local Planning Department, and have a Phase 1 Environmental Inspection by a local environmental consulting company. Within that time period, you have the right to get out of the deal without losing anything but your time. You don't want to buy a building with so many issues that you can't make a profit renovating it.

Preparing the Plans

During the due diligence phase of the contract, try to locate either the original plans or the schematic plans previously drawn for a remodel of the building. In a case where the owner doesn't have any plans, often you will find them in the archives of the planning department. If no plans turn up before you buy the building, then sketch them yourself or hire someone to draw out the existing building with a CAD program after you purchase it. Then you will have the plans for the building in a digital format that will prove helpful not only to you, but also to every future owner and tenant. With these plans, you will know the square footage of the building so as to establish the appropriate rent for each space. You also should be able to see the outlines of the original building beneath the layers of modernizations added over the years, which will help you to assess the rehab needs. When the bank orders an appraisal it will usually include a rough sketch to get the square footage of the property, but this comes after the due diligence process and it is best to have an idea about the building from the beginning.

Consulting the Planning Department

Most states and municipalities have adopted the I.B.C., the International Building Code. This new code makes it much easier to rehab historic buildings than to work with the previous U.B.C., or Universal Building Code. Unfortunately, many of the plans checkers are not familiar with how to use this new code in regard to historic properties. As a result, your plans risk being subjectively or selectively interpreted by the city or county planning staff. Because of this, if the building needs major work to gain an occupancy permit, be sure to have a joint meeting with the planning department, preferably with the head plans checker and a representative of the fire department, before you purchase the building. Be sure to take notes at this meeting and send them to the planning department to assure that they remember and validate what you heard. It is also important to check the records on the building filed at the City or County Planning Department, which may date back 30 or 40 years, to see the history on past renovations or regarding code violations or ongoing disputes. Especially look for any outstanding repairs or improvements that must be done under threat of condemnation.

Phase 1 Environmental Site Inspection

It is best to have a Phase 1 inspection of your building, which will cost around $1,500, only after it is under contract, so as not to lose money. The Phase 1 is handled by environmental engineers, who can be found online or in a phone book. They will locate any asbestos in the building, along with any buried oil or gas tanks. Oil and asbestos can be taken care of through removal; however, an abandoned gas tank, even if it's located on the property next door, is a deal killer unless the seller agrees to have it remediated. Gas travels through the soil and is extremely troublesome and costly to remove. Heating oil tanks, if discovered, are more common and, unlike gas tanks, can be taken care of easily. (Usually the owner pays for this expense before the sale.) The banks will require this Phase 1 on commercial property before they place a loan on it. Sooner or later, you will have to pay for it, so it's best to get any bad news in the beginning.

Beware of "Discoveries": Get to Know the Building

It generally takes 75 days or more to close the transaction on a commercial building. So take your time and think everything through carefully. Make friends with the building ahead of time to avoid any nasty hidden "discoveries," as condition issues are called in real estate jargon, which is why it's so important to meet with the officials of the planning department during the initial due-diligence period. The planning department should be treated like part of the team from the beginning, and usually they are helpful in making the renovation successful. What you look for during the due diligence period are any issues that might make the renovation impossible. If a discovery comes up that looks serious, either negotiate with the seller to fix the issue or lower the price appropriately. Failing those options, get out of the deal. Also be aware that some owners hide costs or write tricky leases with their tenants. These tricks are usually found out by the appraiser and can be used to renegotiate the price downward when found.

Your refusal to move forward on a building purchase can be a negotiating tactic in a case where the owner either didn't tell you or didn't know about a major problem with their building. Often times, upon reflection, the seller will come back to meet your terms, although it might take some time. Once these discoveries are filed in the public records, as in a Phase 1 report, the price of the property will fall. Also, if the landlord is not motivated to repair the issues, the building will continue to depreciate in value, and at some point, the building will be too derelict to rent. This would make it almost impossible for the owner to sell it at any price except the land value less the cost of the demolition.

So what you want to look for is an old building with some condition issues, but still in good enough shape to rent its space to tenants. With this scenario, you stand to get the best buying price on a building and the most value from the renovation for a possible refinance. To be successful, make sure to do your research up front.

Seize the Opportunity

Whenever I complete a renovation project, other developers who were originally interested in buying and restoring the building themselves ask me how I managed to buy it. In most cases, the property had been on the market for months before I found it. When I see a beautiful opportunity to own a building with great potential, I jump on it, and get the building under contract so that I can take a good look at it while it's off the market. What often happens is that prospective buyers are overly cautious about taking a risk, and that fear gets in the way of closing the deal. This is unfortunate. Many of these old buildings fall so far into disrepair that they can't be salvaged, simply because nobody dared to take the leap and give it a try. Without care and attention, an old building becomes an eyesore and an embarrassment to the community, eventually deteriorating until it's a candidate for the landfill. This is a sad loss to all of us, when the building could have been restored to life with the proper attention, again becoming a source of civic pride and a testament to the original founding fathers of the city.

When you find an old building that attracts you to buy it, get it under contract, and then proceed with caution during the due diligence to make sure that it's going to be a smart investment. But don't let too much caution get in the way of missing an opportunity that could turn out to be a very exciting and rewarding experience.

Photographer: Dal Neitzel

The Windsor Hotel. Photo by J.W. Sandison, courtesy of Whatcom Museum.

How to Finance Old Buildings

Photographer: Kate Weisel

Photographer: Kate Weisel

Prospect Street Building, Bellingham, 2015.

Playing the Investment Game

BEFORE I GET INTO THE NUTS AND BOLTS of financing commercial property, I want to share the story of how I first got into the real estate investment business. The idea of investing in commercial real estate was sparked long before I started buying and rehabbing historic property as a profession. In the 1970s, my parents recruited me to find investment property for them, on the strength of my training in architectural engineering and subsequent years working as a carpenter. For inspiration, they handed me a book that has proved to be a classic: *How I Turned $1,000 into One Million in Real Estate in My Spare Time*, by William Nickerson. This book is still a good read today.

Nickerson's book was an epiphany. I suddenly realized that investing in property could be the way to go. Why wait until I'm 55 to invest in rental property so I can retire in my 60s? Why not get started right away? That way, my wife and I could retire early and focus on raising our family. This seemed wise, in view of the fact that it takes time for this type of investment to mature. After that point, it keeps on producing money indefinitely—sort of like have your own personal giant working for you forever. The obstacle to moving forward with this plan was of course that we had no savings to invest. I projected the age of 28 for our retirement. That would give us five years to focus on acquiring enough investment money. We set our goal at $50,000, which was a lot of money in 1976. This cash would be used to buy the largest property that we could leverage with this amount of money.

With this plan shaping in my mind, I searched for property for my parents, who had a sizable savings in the bank to purchase their first real estate. My folks ended up buying two small apartment buildings that gave them a great return on their investment. In the years that followed, I watched the market for promising real estate while helping to manage and fix up these apartments. I looked at dozens of properties and consulted anybody I met along the way who was connected to the real estate investment business.

When I began to search the market for commercial real estate, I was completely open to suggestions and had no difficulty imagining myself as the owner of virtually any property. I was excited by the endless prospects in the real estate section of the newspaper and the commercial brokers listings. With the diverse mix of commercial real estate on the market, I wanted to know which type of property performs best in terms of return on investment. The practical knowledge I gained from that research continues to guide my investment decisions today.

#1 Goal—Maximize the Return on Investment

Finding a property that maximizes the return on your investment is the primary goal for investing in real estate property. The general measure of how to judge an investment property follows the same logic as any good investment strategy. The key question to ask is: What is the yearly return on the original cash spent? Let's take a look at the return for a standard property investment, and then compare the return on high performance property.

Return on a Standard Investment: What to Expect

It is important to note that the standard rate of return applies to property that is not in need of work or distressed in any way. After studying the real estate market, I concluded that a 10% return on your investment is considered satisfactory. At that point in time, 10% seemed to be the point where deals were priced to get investors to put down money. By this standard, if you purchase a property for $100,000 with a 25% down payment of $25,000, you should expect to make around $200 per month.[4] In addition to this cash return, you are saving by paying down the principal on the loan each month, just like putting money in the bank; which in this case, amounts to over $130 on the first month and increases further every month. By taking a depreciation credit on the building, you lower the net income of the property for tax purposes. The loan interest and depreciation expenses increase profits by reducing your taxable income. Since these expenses reduce taxes, the profit they generate is effectively federal income tax free. The owner should also increase rental rates by 2% to 3% each year in order to match average yearly inflation. As previously mentioned, the building's net income determines the property value. Therefore, increasing rental rates to match inflation subsequently increases the property value.[5] So in this case, you would be getting $3,000[6] per year in cash from increased rental income, while also paying down the loan about that

---

4    $200 per month = (25,000*10%) / 12.
5   For example, if a building has income of $10,000 per year, if income increases due to inflation, property value will increase to $103,000 = 3% increase in property value, provided that the expenses do not go up as well.
6    $100,000 x 3% = $3,000.

much per year[7] and increasing the overall value by that much as well. That adds up to a 30% return on your original down payment, much of it income tax free until you sell. This estimate is based on a standard multi-residential investment. Expenses can also be cut if one manages and repairs the apartment units themselves. (This is all spelled out in greater detail in Nickerson's book.)

When you add everything up, the return on your investment is a whopping 30% per year on your original cash investment. If you compare that return rate to the stock market, which claims a 30-year average of 11%, you'll see that this is the way to go in regard to a long-term investment. It is true, as stockbrokers often claim, that property prices increase less over the long term than the stock market. However, this claim fails to take into account the critical point that one can buy that property for only 25% down, or even less; in which case, $25,000 invested in real estate 30 years ago would outperform the stock market by well over double, with the added benefit that your investment would have been made locally, giving you more personal control.

High Performers: Maximizing Your Return

If we can expect to see a 10% return on your original cash down payment in a standard investment, this raises the question, what kind of non-standard real estate performs better? When I first approached a realtor with this question, I was told that I could buy a mobile home park and expect a 20% cash return plus the tax benefits. The drawback with this investment property is that it's not likely to increase in value as quickly, and the pride of ownership might not be as great. If that's the case, then what property gives the highest return on investment? I was surprised to hear the answer: a graveyard. You could expect, after expenses, at least a cool 30% cash return, and that is before depreciation and inflation. In all my years, I've never run across a graveyard for sale, though I never chose to explore the opportunity.

The realtor went on to tell me about the best deal he had ever heard of in his entire career. An abandoned lighthouse located in Oregon on a bluff overlooking the Pacific Ocean had recently come on the market. Apparently, the government had put it up for auction. Several healthy offers came in from people thinking about converting it to a house. But a much higher offer came in from another prospective buyer with a creative idea for the property. The idea was to line the interior walls, including the spiral staircase hall, with a thousand niches that would store miniature crypts containing the ashes of the deceased.

---

7   This is calculated over the life of the loan, usually 25 years.

Limekiln Lighthouse, San Juan Island, Washington. (Not the lighthouse in the story.)

The sale was contingent on getting a zoning variance, as the lighthouse was considered a "special property," and it would require a change of use permit and zoning variance to be converted to a mausoleum.

The new owner succeeded in turning the lighthouse into a mausoleum condo, and priced the urn storage niches according to their location in the building.

Granted, this lighthouse conversion seems far-fetched, not to mention how rare it is to find a lighthouse property on the market. These big-shot brokers, from a major firm in Seattle that deals in only commercial property, were probably having a little fun with us. Whether or not the lighthouse story was true, it's a great example of how you can maximize the return on your investment by being creative. As I have shown, you can also maximize your investment by buying a property that very few people would be interested in owning. That's the beauty of investing in old commercial buildings. But regardless of the investment property you choose, make sure to do your due diligence to avoid getting stuck with a property that won't prove to be a good investment.

Three Golden Rules for Smart Investment

There are three important rules to remember when purchasing a building if you want to maximize your profit. This advice, partly from Nickerson's book, has stuck with me and guided me in making decisions throughout my career.

1. Don't pay too much for a property in the first place to ensure that your investment can increase in value over time.
2. Never sell your property. You make money by purchasing a property, not by selling it. Refinance it and capture the equity tax free for another purchase.
3. Always buy a property that you like in a neighborhood that you enjoy visiting. You won't be selling your building, so make sure to buy a place that you could imagine living in yourself.

Buyer's Remorse: *Learning How to Play the Game*

When I entered the property investment game as a real player, with money to invest, I would soon learn the wisdom of following the "three golden rules." To illustrate their importance, I will share the story of my first investment.

By 1976, my wife and I had succeeded in reaching our goal of saving $50,000. Before moving ahead, we had to pay an accountant to straighten out our tax returns to show the banks and sellers how we made that $50,000. Everything has to be on the up-and-up when you pursue an investment opportunity. In this game, "if you want to play you have to pay" (here *pay* refers to your Federal Income Tax), and now we were ready to play.

We started out by making low-ball offers on anything up for sale that seemed attractive, the larger the better. The Seattle market was ripe with investment property in 1976. Boeing had laid off 55,000 employees and real estate prices were in a free fall. It's hard to believe, but a large brownstone apartment could be bought at that time for less than $10,000 a unit; for example, a 40-unit apartment building on Capital Hill or Queen Ann Hill, now considered exclusive neighborhoods, could be bought for $400,000. To sweeten the deal, the sellers carried the mortgage with a personal contract, as the banks were afraid to lend. However, even with a respectable chunk of cash for investment, my wife and I were the new kids on the block—young and inexperienced, with tax returns dating back only three years. We were not "strong buyers."

When we did get a response from the seller on a highly leveraged offer, somebody connected to the real estate firm would immediately swoop down and get the building under contract for a little bit more and make the buy. As it turned out, the real estate firm was using us as a "stalking horse" to sniff out good deals and then hand them over to better connected clients. After we wised up to this game, we continued to play anyway. It was so much fun simply looking at potential properties, writing up contracts, and getting the feel for negotiating. We liked having the freedom to imagine owning properties without having to commit any of our savings to making an actual purchase. This game continued for over a year until we finally reached a point of frustration at not being able to close on a deal. We were writing up an offer every week and negotiating through the realtors, only to see one property after another drift away.

We ended up buying our first investment property in Bellingham, Washington, not Seattle: a brand new 24-unit apartment building. The way we found the property was pure serendipity. Our car broke down on the way through Bellingham, forcing us to spend a few days in town. While waiting for the car to be fixed, I couldn't help but indulge in my favorite pastime of looking at properties and making offers. Back then I called it "bottom fishing." So I made an offer on the apartment building. To our surprise, the builder and owner of the property bit the hook and pulled us right out of the boat. He sold it to us as quickly as he could. In fact, he left town the same day we closed the deal, right after he got his cash. Most of the big players in the construction and development business during that time went bust and were never heard of again. The owner had given us a fair price on the property, though the building was not well built or located in an up-and-coming neighborhood—two strikes against it.

We were now the proud owners of a large apartment building, our first major property investment. But it wasn't long before a horrible sinking feeling came over us, called "Buyer's Remorse." We had broken Rule #3 in the guide to smart investments by purchasing a property in a rather ugly part of town that we didn't enjoy visiting. Our property didn't appreciate as quickly as would be expected, though we succeeded in making a $20,000 a year profit on our original investment of $35,000. We did okay with Rule #1—Our investment did increase in value. However, credit became very tight with interest rates going up to 18%. Consequently, we could not refinance or sell the property for over ten years. When you're young and ambitious, ten years seems like an eternity. Basically, we were stuck with a property that was not enjoyable to own or manage.

We decided to break Rule #2—Never Sell, because it was such a burden to own this property. We sold the apartment building during a recession, but with only a slight margin of profit, because the building was new and could not be fixed up to increase the value, though it still met the 3% appreciation per year goal. To make the situation still more painful, the person to whom we sold our building held onto it for five years, during which time the rents went up dramatically in the area. The new owner managed to sell it for almost three times what he paid us for it, making a profit of $600,000.

Thankfully, I was still young enough to make the transition from that tough learning experience to move forward with my career. I now had ten years of experience under my belt as the owner and manager of a sizeable property. With this track record, I was in a good position to approach a bank for financing a new property.

Getting a Loan by Purchase Finance Arrangement

To walk you through the steps of purchase financing and explain the terms, I will use the example of my Texas Street Apartment property, for which I received my first bank loan. The procedure for getting this type of loan, irrespective of the property, has not changed in the 35 years I've been putting together my "loan packages."

Going Under Contract

When the seller accepted our offer on the Texas Street Apartment, we were technically under contract. Despite being under contract, the buyer's escrow money[8] usually can be refunded while you complete your contingency agreements. However, if the contingency time runs out before you fulfill the agreements, you the buyer will be "going hard" and you will loose the escrow money if you do not "perform" and buy the property. Up to this point, the procedure for buying a property by purchase finance is the same as the procedure you would use in a residential bank loan. The buyer and the seller sign a contract, which is binding to the seller but not the buyer until he or she removes all the contingencies. Usually it takes one month for the inspection contingency and two months for the financing contingency. Once these contingencies are removed, the seller can lose his escrow money if he or she cannot perform and close the deal.

Leveraging Your Cash

Once the property inspection has been completed, you're ready to arrange financing. In the case of the Texas Street property, we had to come up with only half the down payment, as the seller was willing to carry the remainder as second in the form of a five-year note, requiring full payment in five years. This is called "leveraging your cash": tying up as much property as possible with as little cash outlay up front as possible. Whether or not you succeed in getting the seller to carry the remainder will depend on the situation of the seller. This seller wanted to get the property sold. Often times distressed sellers own distressed properties, so they are more inclined to wheel-and-deal.

---

8   Money held by a neutral third party during a transaction between a buyer and seller. After accomplishing any contingent requirements, the seller most likely will receive the money from the third party.

Justifying the Purchase Price

The next step is for the buyer to secure a bank loan for the remaining amount of the purchase price. For the Texas Street purchase, that figure amounted to 75% of the price. The first part of this process is called "justifying the purchase price."

In private residential real estate, the price of a property remains flexible and depends on many subjective variables. Whereas in commercial real estate, a property is often valued by the Net Operating Income or N.O.I. (the gross income, minus expenses, exclusive of the mortgage payment and depreciation) divided by the prevailing cap rate, or rate of capitalization. The cap rate can change from month to month or city to city. It is based on the selling history of the surrounding property.

If you need financing to purchase a commercial property, you will need to get an appraisal based on 3 years of Profit and Loss (P & L) statements. The P & Ls are used to arrive at the value an appraiser puts on the property. The appraiser determines a pro forma N.O.I. using current and historical P & L statements. The N.O.I. is divided by the cap rate to arrive at the value. Often times, the loan hinges on negotiating the amount of the down payment needed to make the lender feel secure that the building will perform well enough to make the payments, as well as other terms.

The process of getting an appraisal and reaching an agreement with the buyer took about six weeks in the case of the Texas Street Apartments. The reason for the carryover is that all three components are tied together; this is the key to success. The purchase price and the structure of the loan have to be tied to the renovation and the subsequent refinance (although the Texas Street Apartments didn't need renovation). They do not stand alone.

Magic Math Formula

The key to deciding how much to invest in a space—*and this is very import-ant*—is to use this simple formula: Every $10 per month that you increase the rent or lower the building's monthly expenses will increase the appraised value by roughly $1,000. So if you do a $10,000 remodel on an abandoned residential unit, and you can rent it out for $500 per month, the value of the building will increase by $50,000. Or if, for example, you lower the heating cost by $500 by installing a new furnace, you would get the same increase in value. I know this "magic math formula" may seem overly simple, but it has proven true time and time again with my own property investments, and it is an easy formula to remember. I've been told that in today's real estate market this "magic math number" is actually much higher. In 2016, a $10 increase in rent will increase the property's value by $1,600. In view of market fluctuations, I'd recommend using the 10 to 1 formula to give you a basic estimate.

Financing and Refinancing Historic Buildings

The two most important events in the rehabilitation of historic properties are the original purchase of the property, and the eventual refinance of the property after the building has been rehabilitated and fully leased. The purchase price is based on the then-current condition of the property and the rents coming in at the time of purchase. If you negotiate the original building price correctly, and also estimate correctly both the renovation costs and the subsequent increase in rents, at the end of the renovation you should be able to refinance the property and recuperate your original down payment, plus the cost of the rehab; although there will be no income during this process as any profit will be going towards the rehab. By accomplishing this, you will have zero cash in the property and a 25% to 35% equity position in a completely functioning and sturdy building. This is a very attainable 5-year goal. In fact, every facet of the entire project, from the purchase of the building through the rehabilitation and leasing of it, should be focused on achieving a building with this pro forma in mind. This is the underlying strategy to use when you purchase a building, and it cannot be stressed enough.

From the time of my very first building purchase up to my most recent purchase, I have moved my office and warehouse into the building during the rehab process whenever possible. I would recommend this practice. This enables you to be present in the building to supervise the construction, and it gives you plenty of room to work out of. I also sign a long-term lease with my various companies. I, in effect, sign a lease with myself. By doing this, the value of the building will be high when the new appraisal comes in five years later. Generally, I occupy the first rooms rehabilitated, as it is often difficult to lease out the upgraded space for the new higher rent while the remainder of the building is being worked on. Remember that you can write off the rent you pay for your space as a business expense in your taxes, while also showing it as a profit on your new building. This strategy doesn't affect your net bottom line, as the write-off and the profit cancel each other out. Because of this, I suggest you pay yourself the highest rent possible so as to increase the subsequent value of the building.

Capital Improvements

There are specific strategies for keeping the books on this type of property so as to pull out the maximum amount of money when you refinance after the renovation is completed and the building is stabilized. The question that's important to ask here is: How do you put money into the building to fix it up without showing that improvement as an additional expense, and thus lowering the value on the appraisal? The answer is to show the major fix-up costs as "capital improvements." (See IRS website for more information.)

The down side is that you can't deduct these capital improvements as a yearly expense; it's a one-time only event, not a monthly expense. Capital improvements have to be depreciated over a 15- or 20-year period, depending on the type of improvement, so you get to write them off, but over a long period of time. This increases the value of the building because the monthly expenses don't go up. However, the building actually loses money during the years of the renovation. Because of this, give careful thought to the appropriate column for entering your expenses: Will it qualify as maintenance or is it a capital improvement? It's best for your building to have as high of an N.O.I. as possible in the years before the refinance. And make sure to show as much as possible of the renovation as a capital improvement.

Tax Credits

The funds used for major upgrades to the building qualify for tax credits as well. This amounts to 10% of the total money spent that can be deducted from your Federal income tax if the building is over 50 years old, and 20% if the building is placed on the National Register of Historic Places and is part of an approved historic tax credit project. Remember that this write-off applies only to major renovation improvements, not to upgrades such as carpets and new appliances.

Depreciation and Principal Pay Down

The concepts of depreciation and the principal pay down on the loan are also important to understand. These are standard plus and minus aspects to owning any commercial property that are not specific to rehabbing historic properties. Interestingly, depreciation and principal pay down often times balance each other out for tax purposes.

When you buy a building, the terms of depreciation set by the U.S. government enable you to depreciate it over a 32-year period of time. That time period is based on the assumption that a building has a life span of only 32 years.

Let's take the example of a $100,000 building. If the property loses 3% of its value every year for 32 years, at the end of that time it would be worth nothing. This means that the property owner can write off 3% every year for 32 years; in this case, $3,000. This projected life expectancy of a building is hypothetical, and merely a hidden tax incentive or tax loophole to tempt investment in commercial real state. However, the building also has a mortgage when bought. Let's say that the money owed to the bank is $75,000 on a 25-year amortization (which means it will be paid off in 25 years). The rental income taken out of the mortgage payment to pay down the loan balance is counted as profit, which it is, but in the first five or so years of the loan, this principal is roughly around 4%, so it cancels out the depreciation. As the loan matures, this principal will eventually be the entire mortgage payout. For example, let's say it's a 25-year loan. Your payments will stay the same for the entire length of the loan. At the beginning of the repayment period, 98% of your payment goes toward interest; in the last year of the loan, this is reversed and 98% of your payment goes toward principal. So at the end of 25 years, you own the property free and clear.

When to Refinance

In my experience, I've found it best to let the property mature or stabilize until the mortgage on the property is around 50% of the value. That's the time to refinance and pull out the equity. This money is, in effect, not a taxable event, as it is a loan and not considered profit. If you are lucky enough to refinance when interest rates are going down, your mortgage payment will not go up. This is free money. Whereas, if you decide to sell the property, you will have to pay a 21% capital gains tax on the profit; and the original cost of the building will have gone down because you have taken the depreciation. In view of this, it is best to NEVER SELL, unless you do a 1031 Exchange for like property of the same or greater value. Pass on the property to your heirs in your estate. A tax loophole allows your heirs to inherit commercial property with a new "cost basis" equal to its appraised value upon your death. All of the depreciation is forgiven. For this reason, I've often had to wait until the then-current building owners died before the heirs would sell me the property, based on the advice of their accountant and C.P.A. (Certified Public Accountant).

When to Team Up with a Broker

If you're a newcomer to the investment game, I am aware of how this information about financing property could be overwhelming. I was there once myself. But I feel it's vitally important for you to grasp the fundamentals if you want to become a successful investor in commercial real estate. For those of you who want to go beyond the basics of this chapter, consult a detailed guide to help you with the financial picture, or hire some expert advice.

Follow your own instincts as to how much of the process you can handle yourself and when it's wise to consult a financial advisor. I've found that more money can be made from thinking than by labor—in other words, it's best to think everything through carefully and evaluate all of the implications before leaping into an investment or launching a major renovation on a property. Why not let experts handle what doesn't come naturally to you, or that you don't have time to learn, so you can focus on whatever you do best?

Every year, I pay brokers, realtors, and bankers combined over $250,000 for their services. For many years, these fees far exceeded any cash profit I made from my investments. I was tempted to become a real estate broker myself to keep from paying all of these fees. But the truth is that I prefer handling the more creative side of things, and feel it best to stand back from the brokerage business. From my observation, the real estate business creates a mesmerizing effect where a kind of herd mentality sets in. There are many fantastic realtors, but they tend to get caught up in a real estate hothouse scene that follows only the fastest growing trends. As a result, realtors often miss the unique opportunities that pop up from time to time, such as old historic buildings. It's also important to bear in mind that not all realtors are trained in buying and selling of commercial property. Make sure to find a realtor with relevant experience.

Broker fees can be a deal breaker. Many times a deal will fall through because the realtor is more interested in his or her share of the 5% commission than closing the deal. This is true not only of buying and selling but also negotiating the lease, which can add up to a substantial amount. For example, a 10-year $600,000 contract yields a broker fee of up to $30,000 that has to be paid up front. I don't mean to insinuate that realtors are not to be trusted. But it's important that you as the buyer or lessor take a very active role in the negotiations.

Off-Market Buying Strategy: Leveraging the Broker's Fee

When I hear about an attractive property that an owner is thinking of selling, I approach the seller whenever possible, as the seller may be more prone to lower the price by the 5% broker's fee if their bottom line is the same. That 5%, which is always cash off the top, could make all the difference when it comes to closing the deal.

If the property is already listed, I suggest that you contact the listing broker[9] directly. Although the seller will have to pay the broker's fee, the broker will be more likely to push your offer over any others to avoid having to split the fee with another broker. Then make a fair offer up front, knowing what the property will appraise in advance and be ready to move quickly to close, which usually means having the funds available. In this way, the community recognizes you as someone who performs and doesn't waste people's time. Don't get sucked into the game of tying up a property by getting it under contract, and then nickel-and-diming it down through constant discoveries of defects that would warrant a reduced final price tag. If you use the advice in this book, those defects can be spotted up front.

In this chapter on financing commercial property, I have only sketched the topic in broad outlines. An entire book could be written about it. But I hope that my basic guidelines help you to grasp the fundamentals. In many ways, this finance chapter deals with the most boring, but also the most important aspect of renovating historic commercial property. Believe me, when it comes time to have your property appraised for a new loan or to sell all, the subjects touched upon here will become very important. Every $10 that can be shown on the bottom line as increased income will add $1000 to $1600 more to the value of your building. If you keep your eye on this simple fact alone, you will ultimately be successful. Be aware that tax laws and guidelines pertaining to commercial real estate are continuously changing, not just nationally, but regionally as well. This is especially true of historic properties that need to be renovated. So be sure to consult a local tax consultant or a C.P.A. who is skilled in the particular line of work.

My advice to aspiring owners of old buildings is for you to be fair and honest when investing in property. Expect to pay a little more than what you think the building is worth, and expect the renovation to cost a little more than you would believe possible. With a mindset like that, you'll be able to maintain a positive attitude throughout the struggle to close the deal on the property, and will make your investment a success. It's in your best interests to move quickly once you feel comfortable with the property, so make sure not to drag out the negotiations for too long. This type of business is a long-term, big-picture proposition, and it always pays off big in the long run.

---

9   A broker with the contractual right to sell property on behalf of the owner.

Photographer: Kane Hall

How to Restore Old Buildings

Photographer: Kane Hall

Photographer: Kane Hall

Trade Secrets for Easy Renovation

THE NUMBER ONE OBJECTIVE when you renovate an old building is to bring it back to the design of the original architect. If you deviate from that simple goal, your project might spin out of control for many reasons, such as code issues, historic preservation requirements, or problems associated with the building's structure. The best way to avoid getting derailed by such issues is to focus first and foremost on returning your building to its original state when first constructed, and get everything up and running with the existing mechanical systems. Later on, you can replace the plumbing, electrical, and heating systems, which are expensive.

Let's assume that you find a structurally sound building that functions mechanically, meets code requirements, and has the potential to grow your income stream by renovating units that need only new finishes and appliances, or by rehabbing retail or office space already in use in the building that needs only minor repairs. This is the type of building I prefer, as there should be no reason to meet with city officials or the fire department to move forward with the project. This is not to be confused with the building that needs major repairs, in which case, it's important to bring the city and fire department into the discussion before you buy the property. In this chapter I will go over some basic guidelines for doing a standard rehab to help you be as hands-on and efficient as possible when working on improvements in your building. Remember that scaled-down restoration is the key to your success.

Three Rules for Renovation

1. **Keep It as Simple as Possible.**
2. **Keep a Low Profile.**
3. **Take It One Step at a Time.**

Rule #1: Keep It as Simple as Possible

You might ask, how is it possible to do a major rehab of a large building without hiring an architect or an engineer, or having to get a lot of expensive permits to do the renovations?

The answer is: Only tear out all of the "modernization" that has been added over the years, and in the process, the original structure is exposed. This original structure already has everything in the correct place: the supporting walls and other structural members, the plumbing chases, the electrical boxes, and the lighting fixtures.

Before you get started, make sure to study your floor plan to see how the building is structurally supported. If the original supporting structure has been altered, that will determine whether you will need any permits to move ahead with your renovation project.

Building Permits

Generally, to renovate a building that's still in service, you may only need to restore the original finishes. These are the safest projects to work on, from the standpoint of getting the work done without building permits, and without the interference and expense of hiring outside contractors. In my experience, a building permit was only required in the following cases:

- Removing or working on a supporting wall.
- Putting in at least one new electrical circuit.
- Adding new water fixtures such as a sink or toilet.
- Putting in a new heating or cooling system.

You will not need a permit for most cosmetic improvements, unless you are putting in a new electrical circuit or new plumbing, such as in a kitchen or bathroom that requires waterlines, venting, and drains; and providing you are not moving a structural supporting wall or other structural elements.

In some instances, the scale of the renovation will become so grand that you will need to get a demolition permit. For example, in the case of a large retail space from which a lot of material is being removed, you will need to rent and park a dumpster close by the building, which requires a demolition permit. Permits are inexpensive and usually are given over the counter. The permit must be posted in the window so that any public official can see the work inspected. The permit should be the only thing visible in the window. Cover the area around the permit with paper so as not to draw any undue attention to the project.

Rule #2: Keep a Low Profile

When you start to work on a renovation project, keep a low profile. Do as much of the work as possible yourself, or with the help of your own crew. If you take on too much renovation at any given time, it could trigger the need for a permit, which might require you to hire an architect and a structural engineer. Not only are these professionals expensive to hire, but they also have a tendency to expand the scope of the project—not necessarily to make more money, but to protect their legal exposure. In effect, these professionals work for the "other side," and will point out every conceivable code violation and structural hazard to protect themselves from liability issues. Hiring electricians and plumbers to work on the building has the same potential continuances. Often times, they'll use the codes and their familiarity with the city or county building inspectors to expand the scope of the work, and for a building of any size, this can result in hours of labor and a huge bill. In the rehab business, we refer to it as "scope creep." The following story illustrates how easily things can spin out of control if you let a project get out of your own hands.

An Experiment that Proved the Rule

Once I understood the fundamentals of historic rehabs and had a few projects under my belt, I took on the challenge of purchasing and working on several buildings at once. It got to a point where I was looking at so many building prospects that I decided to hire an architect and a private contractor as an experiment. If things worked well, then I could be free from the worry of rehabbing to concentrate on buying and managing properties. I vowed to myself that I would just stand back and watch without interfering in the process.

To be on the safe side, I intentionally picked a smaller project for this experiment—a single-story building, built around 1935, located in downtown Bellingham. I had signed a lease on this property with a hot, new fast-food franchise willing to pay over $24 per sq. ft. per year. More important, this new business was likely to generate enough foot traffic to drive away the transients and miscreants that had taken over the corner. The plan was to put the restaurant into the corner 1,200 sq. ft. retail space, and add a series of large windows along a 50-foot solid wall to give the area a new identity. Because of this large expanse of blank wall space, the area had become a prime location for negative social behavior. It dragged down the neighboring businesses, especially the retail spaces located in this building, not to mention the buildings down the block. This property was one of the prominent corner buildings in this part of town, so fixing it was key to the success of the entire area.

The project began with a big hoopla in the press, as this was the first franchise to open in the downtown since the mall opened in 1988. Due to the building's location in a busy retail area, the contractor installed a security fence down the middle of the sidewalk around the site. Unfortunately, the architect and contractor both made an incorrect assessment for the construction of the wall, and drew up the plans and got the permit based on this mistake. The contractor and the architect had wrongly assumed that the wall was made of concrete and masonry; however, two feet above the concrete at the lower section of the wall, they discovered wood frame construction. The mistake was discovered on the first day, and an engineer was called in to remedy the problem. I just stood back and watched.

It soon became apparent that this project was the engineer's first job on a historic building. First she checked the concrete footings. They had been poured in a hand-dug ditch, which was common practice at the time of the building's construction. The engineer informed me that the entire foundation of the 6,000 sq. ft. building had to be re-poured to modern specifications. The structural engineer assigned to this job explained that she had a "fiduciary responsibility" to report this issue to the city officials. The construction was halted and, as if that weren't enough, the electrical contractor hired by the general contractor told the "Team" that because the restaurant would require the 100-amp service to be replaced by 150-amp service, the electrical room had to be abandoned and rebuilt or provided with a new entrance door no further than 15 feet away from it. Moving this room was next to impossible, and the other option would require getting an easement from the neighboring bank to access the door from their parking lot; also virtually impossible to get, as national banks don't seem to have the capacity to look at such issues. So the project was stalled and the entire mess collapsed back onto my shoulders.

If I had continued the rehab process at this pace, the simple storefront renovation of only one of the six retail spaces would have cost more than the purchase price of the building. The architect and the contractor didn't care to risk their ongoing relationship with the planning department over a code issue on my behalf. There was no incentive for them to restrict the scope of the work, as they get paid by the hour; so the more difficult the project gets, the more money they stand to make. Not that the contractors, the architect, or the structural

engineer had any such intentions from the start. Apparently, they had never restored a historic building, and they were not prepared for the "discoveries," as these unexpected code upgrades are called in rehab work.

When the contractor walked away and the architect was no longer needed, I had no choice but to jump back in and handle the project myself. First, I talked to the owner of the engineering company and had the novice removed from the job site. I resolved the financial issue by hiring an electrical company that would not try to turn a $1,000 job into a $25,000 job though a reckless manipulation of the codes. I had my own crew install the windows. This relatively simple job tied up that corner of the street for over six months. The lesson I learned from my experiment with outside contractors is that this type of renovation work requires expertise and finesse, which are hard to acquire, and take years of experience. I now appeared to be the expert in town at restoring historic properties with a limited budget. From this point forward, I controlled the renovations as much as possible.

Although it was a painful learning experience, this project turned out to be highly successful. With its attractive new wall of windows overlooking the street, this corner building was no longer the preferred "hang out" spot.

The fast-food restaurant that moved into the building drew crowds, and the sales in the surrounding retail stores picked up dramatically. I owned several other buildings in the neighborhood, and those retail businesses, as well as the other retailers along the block, benefited greatly from this change on the corner. Because the retailers did well, so did the landlords of the buildings. My investment in this building paid off. The total rent collected on this particular space was around $550 per month when I purchased the building. The newly renovated space brought in over $2,200 in rent per month. By using my simple math formula, $10=$1,000, the value of the building increased by over $150,000, which was about what it had cost to renovate the building when the dust finally settled on this project.

As my story illustrates, rehabbing an old commercial building is considerably more challenging than remodeling an old house. The codes are stricter, the scale is much grander, and there are far fewer professionals who are trained to do this kind of work. Unless you live in a large city that can command the high rents that will afford you the luxury of hiring professionals, the owner of a historic building must be as hands-on as possible. I don't want to discourage you from getting into the historic rehab business—far from it. These old buildings are crying out for our help. My intention is to show you that it is possible to be quite successful in this business, if one is careful from the beginning.

Rule #3: Take It One Step at a Time

When you start a renovation project on a building, go through the spaces one at a time. Break the rehab into smaller individual projects. My most successful rehabs took over five years to complete. The Daylight Building, which is our most successful project to date, took us twelve years. By the end of the project, every part of the building had been completely gone through, and the necessary renovations triggered only a handful of permits for minor structural alterations and mechanical repairs.

If parts of the building are vacant, especially storefronts, start by working on one of those areas first. In a situation where a tenant occupies the building, you will have to wait until the tenant moves out or the lease expires to work on that space. If possible, do all of the work as a Capital Improvement, for tax purposes.

Do-It-Yourself Guidelines: *Tricks of the Trade*

You can make a dramatic improvement to an old building and keep your expenses to a minimum by doing most of the work yourself. The key to your success is that everything you need to transform your property from a neglected or defaced building into a historic restoration with original character is right there in the building. For the most part, it's simply a matter of revealing what's hidden beneath the surface layers added onto the building over the years.

With the advent of the electric light bulb and electric fan at the turn of the century, it was no longer necessary for architects to design rooms with large windows and high spacious ceilings to allow for natural light and airflow. The trend was to lower the interior ceiling height and cover up the clearstory windows rising above the awning on the façade. The windows facing the street in the lower part of the building, especially windows facing the alley, were bricked in for security reasons. Two of my favorite tricks for renovating a building are to remove the modern façade and tear down the lower ceiling. These changes make a dramatic immediate improvement to the exterior and interior of the space without much cost, as everything needed for the makeover is already there for you to use.

Restoring the Façade

Transforming a building to its original character by reviving the façade is one of the easiest and most satisfying aspects of a historic renovation. In the old commercial buildings on the market, you'll often find that the structure has been modernized with a new front. By simply tearing off the added material, the original front is again exposed to the public. It's easy to remove, because in the interests of saving time and money, the

Photographer: Kane Hall

developer often framed over the original front of the building with cheap material such as plywood or plaster over a metal grid.

Restoring the Clearstory

The clearstory was a distinctive feature of the commercial buildings pre-dating electricity. This decorative set of windows above the front door allowed light to penetrate into the interior of the building for daily business. Architects took great care to make the design of these windows aesthetically pleasing, and not merely functional. After electric lighting was in common use, the favorite modernization method of architects was to lower the ceiling level to conceal the newer mechanical systems. The clearstory windows as well as skylights were covered up in these types of redesign. This modification worked well to accommodate the electrical light and heating systems from a mechanical perspective. But to my mind, it was a disaster in terms of the loss of aesthetic beauty and proportion, not to mention that natural light is superior to artificial light. When you strip off the modern façade and remove the hung ceiling, you will have access to the original clearstory, which will add height and bring more light into the building.

Restoring the Windows

Windows are a key feature of the original architecture of these old buildings. It's important to bring them back into use to restore the building's integrity. Typically, the windows facing the alley in these old buildings were blocked up with bricks. It is surprisingly easy to remove the bricks, put the replacement window back into the already formed opening, which is pre-engineered to fit a window or door, and cover it with a metal security grating. This not only lets natural light into the rear of the building, but it also allows for airflow. To preserve the historic character, I recommend keeping the original windows whenever possible, unless the building is located in a very cold climate, in which case a thermal window might be installed to reduce the heating expenses. Thermal pane glass in windows of any great size, such as the front display windows, should be avoided, as it tends to cloud up, despite what the manufacturers say, and is very expensive to replace; instead use ½-inch plate safety glass when possible.

The original wooden frames have a distinctive charm, and it's more economical to refurbish the old windows than to replace them with new ones. They can be taken apart, cleaned up, and re-hung with new rope. Caution should be used when sanding or scraping old paint, as it is almost always lead based. Be sure to get the upper window working properly again, not just the lower one. Unfortunately, in many of these older buildings, the windows and frames have

rotted with age and have to be replaced. If the building is listed on the historic registry, you will have to install wooden windows with insulated glass—an expensive proposition, as new wooden windows have to be custom made. I usually have one of my men fabricate the wooden windows from scratch in my basement work area, which, by the way, is how many of them were made in the first place, not in a factory, but on the job site.

Revealing the Old Ceiling

Restoring the old ceilings in the interior of a building is surprisingly easy to accomplish. Several of my buildings have had two or more hung ceilings put in as a way of concealing the new mechanical systems, such as heating ducts, wiring, and plumbing. Things were done on the cheap, and the contractors and former owners throughout the years just covered up the last remodel with a new one.

The average ceiling height of the larger historic retail spaces is around 14 to 18 feet. When a retail space is opened up to its original height, the room regains its true proportions. In most cases, as mentioned, tearing down the hung ceiling will also expose the original clearstory window, which is often still usable. Since these original features of the architecture already exist, to make this major improvement is inexpensive. It can be accomplished with only a simple crow bar and a demo permit. The joy of tearing down a hung ceiling to reveal the original one hidden underneath is intense, because this transformation happens so quickly. You can sense the building breathing freely again.

Restoring the Old Floors

The original floors of old buildings are often interesting and add a lot of character to an interior space when refurbished. The subflooring in buildings built before the 1940s (before the use of plywood) is usually good quality wood, suitable to be refinished, such as a tongue-and-groove 3- to 4-inch fir. Often times, this subflooring was covered with a tongue-and-groove hardwood such as oak or maple. In all these cases,

with a little bit of experimentation, you can learn how to finish these floors with a rented machine and seal with a non-toxic, water-based sealer. So here again, what you need for your historic upgrade is already in the building: the flooring material is buried underneath carpeting or linoleum, which is easy to remove. These refinished floors invariably look almost new, and the cost to install them again would be very expensive.

Restoring the Walls

The walls in historic buildings are usually constructed of lath and plaster. Under this lath and plaster on the exterior facing wall and on the main interior supporting walls, you will find brick or stone. This construction gives you a great opportunity to take the wall down and expose the underling brick or stone. Even though these masonry support walls were not meant to have a finished appearance when originally built, the material can be wire brushed, repointed if necessary, and then sprayed with a clear fixer to protect the mortar from flaking. Be careful to repoint the bricks with a soft sand mortar. Do not use cement with bricks, as bricks need to breathe. This exposed brick element adds character to the space, whether it be retail, office, or residential. This relatively simple and inexpensive upgrade was there all along, just like the floor.

When repairing the lath and plaster you have two choices: You can remove it entirely, which will allow you to put in new conduit wiring and modern plumbing, and then cover it with 5/8-inch sheet rock. Or you can cover it with 1/4- or 1/2-inch sheet rock. This works for the ceilings as well, which can be finished smoothly. For a renovation that requires new wiring or plumbing, I usually tear it all out, and then I can be done with it. Otherwise, the cracks will never stop forming, as lath and plaster often times doesn't patch up like modern dry wall, and the repairs can become problematic in the future.

A word on asbestos. Be careful to test the plaster to be sure it doesn't contain asbestos, which was commonly used in many construction materials, including plaster, as a flame retardant in old buildings. Flooring tiles were also commonly made with asbestos up to 50 years ago. Because you are the owner, with proper training, it is legal in some places for you to personally remove and dispose of asbestos insulation on pipes as well as asbestos tiles on smaller jobs.

Roof Repair

Most of these historic buildings have a flat, hot-tar roof with layers and layers of tarpaper and black tar, sometimes four inches thick, as over the years, the owners just keep putting down more and more coats of the tar paper. These roofs are problematic. When moisture gets inside, it steams its way out in the hot summer, and causes the tar to crack in the winter when the moisture freezes, which causes the cracks to leak when the roof thaws out. These tar roofs are rarely put down now. We usually replace them with a membranous material, which is light and easy to put down and repair. If you don't have the funds to replace the roof immediately, there is an economical short-term alternative. You can put an emulsion on the existing roof every summer, usually the white reflective type. The long-term solution is usually expensive: $10 per sq. ft., and the process is more complicated. It requires you to remove all the old tar material down to the diagonal 1 x 8-inch fir planking and cover it with plywood; then cover the plywood with a 3-inch insulation; and finally, cover the insulation with a plastic vinyl membrane material glued on the seams.

In recent projects, I have had success with pumping insulation material into the crawl space between the ceiling and the roof, and then going over the tar, no matter how thick, with this vinyl material. I now have my own crews do this work, and the cost is about $3 per sq. ft., including the insulation.

Upgrading the Mechanical

Now we are ready to discuss the not-so-glamorous aspects of historic renovation. The mechanical aspects of a building are equally as important, and sometimes more important, to the success of a renovation project as its beautification. Often, it is the failure or impending failure of the roof or the boiler that forces an owner to sell a property. In the mind of the owner, the "old horse" was dying and needed to be sold. So don't be surprised to find that virtually every aspect of the building you've bought is compromised mechanically, as it was only functioning well enough to keep it alive. I will walk you through the main mechanical aspects involved for maintaining a building and offer some advice about what you can do yourself.

Treat the mechanical parts of the building the same as you would the rest of the renovation: take care of them one at a time, and, if possible, spread the work out over years. For example, it might take five years of repeatedly patching a roof until you can afford to refinance the building to pay for a new roof.

The Boiler

Let's start with the boiler, because I have found that old buildings usually have a steam or hot-water boiler system. In some cases, you will find a boiler built for coal that was converted to oil and then to gas over the years; this type of boiler is very inefficient and should be replaced. The potential savings from upgrading the boiler can pay for its cost. Check to see if money to cover the expense of the conversion is available through your local energy companies—in this case, the gas company. Calculations will be made as to the savings and the gas company will loan the money to you to replace the old boiler; the monthly savings will pay for the new furnace. In this way, you get a new dependable energy efficient boiler, which is paid off in 10 years or so at no additional cost to you. Otherwise, wait until funds are available through a refinance.

If you are fortunate enough to have one of these hot-water radiant heating systems in working condition, do your best to save it. They are cheaper than other heating systems; they are quiet; they do not burn or start potential fires; and they emit a consistent steady heat. On the down side, the individual tenant's cost to heat their space cannot be billed to them with a central heating system, unless it's worked out in the triple-net lease for commercial tenants per sq. ft. or built into the rent for residential units. Often, I find it best to put in a modern heat-pump, heating-cooling unit with separate meters in the larger retail spaces, and keep the hot-water radiant heat for the residential spaces. This allows the commercial tenants to control their heating and cooling system. Another plus is that a system like this makes the renovated space seem modern, especially with the high ceilings and exposed circular metal vents.

When dealing with heavy cast-iron radiant heaters, be sure to replace the shut off valves so that your tenants can adjust the heat themselves. Nothing is more distressing than to drive by your building in the winter and see windows open in a unit because the radiator cannot be closed down when the room gets

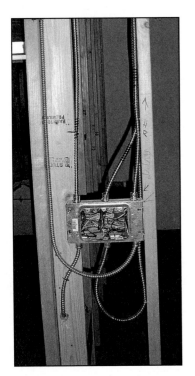

too hot. Usually, there is only one thermostat in the building, and it is located in the common hallway where there is no heater. So care has to be taken to control this situation. I keep the thermostat turned down reasonably low, unless someone complains. In that case, I give the tenant a small, plug-in electric oil heater.

Electrical

Fortunately, in commercial spaces and even in smaller apartments, it is approved by code standards to put the electrical wires into conduit (the small metal pipes externally mounted on the walls through which the wires are pulled). Eventually, this conversion should be done, as banks and insurance companies frown upon the old knob-and-tube method as a fire hazard. The old method, in which the positive and negative current is separated and strung from porcelain posts through the walls and floor, was the only way that electric wires were installed up until the Second World War. The new conduit is not very attractive, but considering the difficulty of putting the wires back into the walls, it's the only solution that makes sense in terms of cost. Also important, the old screw-in fuse boxes should be replaced by boxes with circuit breakers. Only a licensed electrician can do this work.

When it comes to replacing the fixtures in retail spaces, the original schoolhouse lighting that was typically hung from the 18-ft. ceilings looks the best, but it can be expensive to replace. You'll find that the hung fixtures made for factories, which are still in common use, look almost as good as the original glass ones, and they cost less than half the price. Both schoolhouse and factory reproduction fixtures can be found online at various Internet retailers for a reasonable price.

Plumbing

Now on to the plumbing maintenance, and good luck with that. It's difficult to replace plumbing from 100 years ago that's buried in the floor and walls. But eventually, it all needs to be replaced. Unlike the electrical wiring, the water pipes and drains cannot be externally mounted to the walls and ceilings. In several of my buildings, I have had to replace everything at one time, which requires opening up the walls and ceilings and then covering them back up.

Do the repairs yourself, to the greatest extent possible, until you have acquired enough property to afford to hire someone trained in this field to help. You don't want to pay a licensed plumber to patch a torn out wall. Remember, you only need to replace what has worn out; you're not installing anything new but pipes. For new construction, such as a new bathroom or kitchen, you'll need a professional plumber and a building permit. I use a professional pipe router, similar to a Roto-Rooter, for plugged drains. But eventually the pipes might crack, and at that point, they'll have to be replaced.

These days, with 25 properties and counting to manage and maintain, I want to hire as many skilled workers with plumbing skills as possible to get between my 500 toilets and me.

Fixtures

If the bathtubs and sinks are badly stained, they can either be refinished in place or taken to a shop and sprayed with a new finish. Keep the original fixtures, if possible, as they seem to last forever. If they're not salvageable, replacements can be found in secondhand stores or recycling centers that specialize in old building materials. When it comes to toilets, it's best to replace an old toilet with a modern one that uses less water. Your community might have a program to conserve water, which will help pay for the new toilets, much like the gas company's arrangement for the furnace. You can pay a little more for reproductions or a considerable amount more, if you want to keep an authentic look. On the other hand, a modernized bathroom can do a lot to dispel a negative bias that a prospective tenant may have about old buildings as far as sanitation and efficiency are concerned.

Upgrades such as a modern heating system, a new breaker box, and new kitchen appliances are modernizations that do not detract from a historic property. Instead, these improvements help to convey the impression that this old building will be here for another 100 years.

Key Lessons:

- Remember the #1 Goal: Restore the building to its original look and feel.
- Get the building working mechanically, and eventually add new mechanical systems.
- Keep a low profile to avoid permits and costly "scope creep."
- Work on the rehab one space, one issue at a time.
- Keep it simple and focus on the essential upgrades first.
- Repair rather than replace worn architectural features.
- Splurge on the façade. The image of a building that has declined takes many years to restore. It's best to kick that around quickly and give your building a great start.
- Treat the cosmetic features of the building restoration, such as doors, floors, and painting, as you would in restoring an old house. Just use common sense.

How to Manage Old Buildings

Guidelines for Successful Management

MORRIS PHIA, a very successful inner city developer, once pointed out that the term "landlord" is a misnomer in our business. "We're in the shit eating business," Phia said humorously. We are far from the days of yore when tenants served their lord and master. The roles have reversed. Today's landlords are actually in the service industry and should be as accommodating to their tenants as possible. Phia made his point in reference to the owner of a building that defaulted on his loan because he had failed to understand this concept. Although the owner had been fortunate in finding great tenants to lease his building, he interfered with their success by dictating how they should run

Photographer: David H. Johnston

their businesses. The landlord should very seldom take an aggressive posture; instead, the landlord should listen to and try to resolve the tenants' complaints and issues.

#1 Goal: Focus on Your Tenant's Success

As the owner and landlord of a building, you can only expect to prosper if your tenants are successful themselves. To make this happen, it's important to encourage your tenants to feel in control of their leased space in the building. Let them enjoy a sense of ownership and freedom.

Whereas the landlord of the building should be thinking long-term, say ten years out into the future of the property, the retail and office tenants have to stay focused on the day-to-day concerns necessary to make their businesses work. They are on the front line every day in that location. Keeping your tenants' success foremost in mind and helping to assure the prosperity of their businesses should be your primary goal.

This also applies to leasing space to tenants in the residential units of multi-use commercial buildings. These tenants should be encouraged to "own" their personal space while also feeling part of a residential community.

You want your tenants to take pride in their rental space, and take care of that space. It's your job to make sure that your building is attractive, clean, and well managed at all times. Many of the old commercial buildings that I restored over the years were not managed properly when I first acquired them; several of my properties were not managed at all. Poor management directly impacts the image of the building and the way the tenants treat their rental space. In cases of serious negligence, years of consistent attention will have to be allotted to a building to get the energy flowing in a healthy way. But from that point forward, the building will take on a new personality, which will attract like-minded tenants to rent the space.

It took many years to figure out the correct approach to renting out previously distressed and poorly managed properties. But now that I've worked out effective management practices that work with the cooperation of my tenants, I'm very keen on buying old buildings designed for mixed commercial/residential use.

In the following section, I'll walk you through the process of managing the commercial and residential space of your property, with the hope that your experience as a landlord will go smoothly from the start.

Managing Your Commercial Space

Renting Out Commercial Space: First Steps

When a rental space in your building becomes vacant and you want to lease it, follow these simple guidelines commonly practiced in commercial real estate.

1. **Prepare the advertisement.** Write out a one-page description of the rental space mentioning rent per sq. ft., any triple net charges, which might include common area maintenance, insurance, roof maintenance, janitorial services, and water service. This is the information that you will include in your ad for Craigslist or the newspaper, or give to brokers for advertising purposes, provided you are prepared to pay a 5% brokers fee.

2. **Request a Letter of Intent.** When a person shows interest in a space, ask the prospective tenant for a L.O.I. (Letter of Intent), along with their business plan and a personal financial statement. Once you have these three items, you can better assess the tenant's chance of success. Most businesses should have a realistic amount of cash to put into the inventory and infrastructure of the new business. Also, and even more important, the tenant's projection of income and costs should account for a least a one-year period where they expect to either lose money or just break even. Renting out space to an undercapitalized business sets up both parties for a potentially negative experience.

   With the L.O.I. and supporting documents, you can write a response letter working out the details of the new lease as to term length and price; these negotiation letters can go back and forth until you and the tenant reach an agreement. By writing out the terms and conditions, there can be no confusion as to what was agreed to.

3. **Secure the Lease.** You as the landlord will be signing a contract that requires the prospective tenant to fulfill rent payments for the period of time stated on the lease. Unless there is a jump clause in the lease, allowing you or the tenant to get out of the lease, the tenant and the landlord are in a relationship for the entire lease period, whether their business is successful or not. Conversely, the tenant has first possession

of the space unless he breaks his lease agreement by not paying rent, or due to some other breach of the terms specified in the lease even if the building is sold. To ensure that your tenant is prepared to cover the rent for the entire period, make sure that the tenant has the ability to secure the lease amount with hard assets such as a personal home or savings account. You then can attach a lien to their assets in case of a default in the rent payment. If the tenant has to terminate the business or chooses to move out of the rental space for any reason, then the pressure is on the tenant to sell their business with the lease agreement or find a new tenant to lease the space; either way, you are covered.

One point to remember with leasing commercial space is that it's the responsibility of the tenant to repair and replace everything in the interior, including the exterior window, unless otherwise stated. This includes the heating system, if it is used solely for their space, and the bathroom and the electrical system. Make sure that your tenants are aware of their responsibility from the start, by pointing it out in the lease. Otherwise, this can be a source of confusion, because in the case of a residential lease, the landlord is responsible for taking care of everything, not the tenant.

4. **Provide flexibility in the terms of the lease.** When negotiating a new lease, keep the big picture in mind: the potential value of your building is directly related to the rent. In other words, the appraisal value of your building is based upon the length of the leases and the amount of rent collected from the tenants. Be generous in the terms you set with your tenant at the beginning of the lease, since that is the period when the tenant will be committing a lot of resources to improving their new space and buying inventory. It's in your best interests as well to help your new tenant to be a success. You want tenants to rent from you on a long-term basis to stabilize your income and increase your property's value.

The Escalator. I recommend starting your new tenants with a contract arrangement that I call the "escalator," which has proved to be a win-win over the years. The rent price is gradually escalated as the new tenant's business grows. In the first year, give your tenant a month or two rent-free, and a 50% discount for the subsequent couple of months. Perhaps at the start of the second year, you could offer another month rent-free. Be sure to work in a 3% yearly increase over the term of the lease so that at the end or year one, they will be paying full rent, and by the end of a five-year lease, the rent will have increased by 16%.

You'll want to think about the implications of these escalating rent arrangements for a refinance of your property. When the appraiser and the bank set a new value on the building, they will only look at the rent figures in the lease and will not take into account any money spent on T.I.s (Tenant Improvements), or any loss incurred from temporary rent-free arrangements at the beginning of the lease. So structure a plan that enables all of the leases in your building to stabilize at about the time of the refinance, usually every 5 to 7 years.

Option to switch leases. Because I own properties of all sizes and locations in the downtown, I will work with my tenants to switch leases if they choose to move to a different location in town or want to lease a larger or smaller sized space. The best-case scenario for this option is a situation where a retail or office tenant wants to expand. In that case, it's a win-win to move them to a larger vacant space when possible. It is also advisable to help a tenant downsize when necessary, but first try to rent their space to a new tenant so that no rent is lost in this transaction and they are helped out of a jam. It's no fun to go after a bad debt to collect from somebody already in trouble. Always help out your tenants in any way possible.

I want to point out, once again, that anything a property owner/landlord can do to create a healthier business for the tenant is not only good for the tenant; it's also good for the owner of the building and for the downtown in general.

Balancing the Building's Energy

The best way I've found to approach management is to view a building as a unique entity with a personality of its own. When you view the building you manage as a living entity, you will understand how to correct issues and balance the flow to make the building function as a whole.

Lead Tenant Policy

Whether you own several commercial properties in a city, or just one building, make sure to observe the lead tenant policy. When you lease a building, there should always be one lead tenant. That tenant will help to set the tone and image for the building and give it an identity. Choose an attractive business such as a restaurant, a clothing store, or a flower shop as your lead tenant.

> Visualize your building as a living entity and balance the energy flow in the building.

Once that tenant is established, never move a competing business into the building unless the lead tenant approves of your decision. Not only would it be unfair to the existing tenant to bring in unwanted competition, but it could create so much tension between the two tenants that the other businesses in the building would suffer as well. This is important to consider when shifting tenants from one location to another. Inevitably when renting commercial property, tenants will move in and out and shift the building's energy.

Maintaining a strong lead tenant helps to stabilize the flux, as the public often identifies the building with the lead tenant. For example, my Daylight building has a flower shop located on the main corner with a coffee shop attached. In summertime, the owners place pots of flowers in front of the shop as well as on the tables outside the coffee shop. This gives the building a pleasant gentle look from the street, and the tenants who rent the residential units upstairs feel and act accordingly. This tenant has been there so long and given the building such a good vibe that I intentionally do not raise their rent. In fact, the rent has been lowered, as flower shops have to compete with large retail chain stores and have suffered greatly and I did not want to lose them as a tenant.

Good Retail Mix = Good Energy

To balance the tenants' energy flow in the building, there should be a healthy mix of various retail shops on the ground floor. I've found it beneficial to lease to a tenant with some kind of food service venue, such as a coffee shop or a full restaurant. If there is at least one kitchen cooking for the general public in your building, this makes it feel more like a home.

The St. Helens Inn property, featured in the first part of the book, is a good example. It was hard to attract worthy tenants for the 55 residential units in the building because the ground floor shops were not the right mix. There was a motley crew of retail businesses, dominated by a casino. To resolve this problem, I leased the master 7,000 sq. ft. space occupied by the casino to a large bakery and cut the new tenants' rent in half to tempt them into the building. The aroma of the bakery permeating the building helped to transform the negative perception of the St. Helens. Now it is viewed as a homey, comfortable place to live.

Managing Your Residential Units

Practically everything I would ever need to know about residential management I learned with my first commercial property, the Texas Street Apartments in Bellingham. After I bought the property and lived there one year, I hired a manager to oversee the apartments while I took a six-month working vacation. On my return, I found that the manager had started pocketing an amount of the rent money each month, starting at $50 and reaching $300. To make matters worse, ten of the units had been rented to members of a teenage motorcycle gang—nothing like the Hell's Angels, thank goodness, but an amateur startup club made up of misguided youths, with Honda 150s and matching tattoos inscribed on their wrists. The kids repaired their motorbikes in the living room. The gang leader had collected garbage in the kitchen for the entire winter. Many of the original tenants had moved out of the apartment building because of the commotion caused by the club members, and when they moved out, another teenager moved in.

The best solution was to become their mentor and help the kids transition to a property better suited to their lifestyle. I found a rundown farm out in the country, and hired them to work on the apartment building in exchange for their damage deposit for the farm. I organized their older relatives to help with the move and sign the lease. I also returned a portion of their damage deposit for tearing out the carpets in their units and hauling it away. I did all of this to avoid a potentially ugly confrontation with a forced mass eviction, but also to help these kids move along.

Now we routinely do a credit and criminal check on the potential tenants of our rental properties to avoid this kind of situation. We also strive to achieve a compatible tenant mix when screening tenants for placement in a building, and we assure that all of our properties are maintained with a standard of cleanliness that gives our tenants a sense of pride in their place of residence and supports their well being.

Maintain High Standards

Here is my rule of thumb for renting old commercial buildings (which also applies to purchasing a building): Don't rent out a building that you would not feel comfortable living or working in yourself, if not at the present time, earlier in your life—as a college student, for example. That means facilitating a clean and safe environment with all appliances in good working order for the tenants. It also means maintaining the condition of every interior and exterior feature of the building to give it a positive image in the community.

Give Your Building a Positive Identity

The first commercial building with a residential component that I purchased was the Helena Building in Bellingham, described in the first part of the book. The clientele living in the old hotel space on the second floor gave the building a serious image problem. The owner was leasing the entire "hotel" to a third party when I acquired the property. The total rent collected for the entire 10 units was only $400. To my surprise, since we renovated the Helena building and made it clean and attractive, even with the shared "European plan" bathrooms, the apartments are always filled with tenants. Besides the "pensioners," the single, middle-aged men who lived there when I bought the building, we now rent to college students and young adults who love the Helena for the authentic historic character of this building. Living in these economy units from a previous age is now considered chic and exciting.

The transition to the Helena's new identity and clientele took several years to complete. It takes a steady, involved management style to establish a new order. After that point, the building has seemed to take care of itself, as the new tenants live in such close proximity that they watch out for each other. At first, we hired a manager to live on the premises and oversee the building, but now we are able to manage this once-troubled complex from our main office.

Upgrade Common Areas

The key to giving the space a fresh, more positive identity was to add new finishes and appliances and update the common areas, such as the entrance hallways and bathrooms. I always install a laundry room in my apartment buildings, which creates a homier atmosphere in a building complex. Coin operated washing and drying machines also provide an added source of income. There are companies that will install the machines for free and pay the owner of the building a small amount for managing them. I have found it best for my company to buy and service these commercial machines. It's surprising how much money they can make (here, once again, increasing the value of the property by the $1=$100 formula).

Build Controls into the Leasing Process

1. **Background Check.** In Bellingham, where my company manages 108 residential spaces, we do a credit and criminal check on all prospective tenants, for which they pay a fee when they fill out the application. If the applicant/prospective tenant proves to have bad credit or no credit history, then a responsible party such as a parent is required to sign on the lease.

2. **Check-in/Check-out List.** There is a rather long and detailed check-in and check-out list so that all damages and imperfections are noted at move in, so that at move out all the damages can be noted and paid for out of the damage deposit, which is equal to the last month rent. By law, the damage deposit has to be held in a separate account from the rent revenue.

3. **Control the Lease Period.** My residential properties are always full in Bellingham, primarily because it's home to Western Washington University with its large student population. To avoid vacancies in the summer months, a common problem in university towns, the lease period for all our residential units begins in September and extends for at least one year. This policy helps to attract students who want to remain in Bellingham throughout the year, eliminating the problem of vacancies during the summer months.

Off-Site Management: Pros and Cons

Because we manage the Bellingham properties ourselves, we can be very quick at repairing and fixing minor problems such as plumbing leaks. In other cities in Washington, where I own over 80 residential units, we must rely on independent management companies and private contractors to do repairs and make any major improvements. This insulates the owner from the day-to-day grind and responsibility of ownership; however, hiring workers through off-site management companies has proven to be very expensive when compared with doing the work myself. And when it comes time to refinance, this additional expense cuts into the value of the building.

KEYS TO SUCCESSFUL MANAGEMENT

Cooperation, Respect, Communication

To assure the sustainability of your building for the long haul, it is important to instill a spirit of cooperation and ownership among your tenants. Remember that your building is a living thing and your tenants are its eyes and ears. If the tenants are proud to be living and working in their rental space, they will take ownership of the building and it will virtually run on its own. For this to happen, the owner and his managers have to know what is going on in the building on a daily basis. If the residential component of the building has over 10 units, there should be an on-site manager or a least one long-term tenant with close ties to the management. Steady rapport should be kept up with the other tenants as well. I now rely on my janitors to give me the day-to-day vibe as far as what's going on in my buildings. Your goal in management should be to maintain a building in excellent working order to the satisfaction of your tenants. If the owner is proud of the building, then it is easier for the tenants to take pride in it as well.

Conclusion

The Future of Old Buildings

A S I HAVE ILLUSTRATED throughout this book, the majority of old buildings constructed of heavy timber and masonry, before the era of modernization, have aesthetic proportion and great durability, factors that make them well worth the effort to preserve. Unfortunately, the modern trend continues to dominate commercial building in our cities, even though the modern structures in our urban environment, in my estimation, lack character and style compared with pre-1920s architecture. We've learned through hindsight, however, that the materials and construction methods used for the sake of easy, affordable building solutions and rapid development often do not hold up over time. The projected life span for these structures is, at the most, 70 years until demolition. Our cultural mindset of disposability has encouraged this unsustainable practice in the building industry. It's time for us to embrace the wisdom of our forefathers, who built their commercial buildings to last for many generations.

It is highly important to appreciate the historical significance of this commercial architecture. These old buildings give an architectural anchor to our short historical past relative to Europe and other countries with centuries of development. This is especially true in western states such as Washington and Oregon, developed late in the 19th century when American settlement expanded to the farthest frontier. Not only do the restored historic buildings in our cities add a sense of time and place to the urban environment, they work well with modern high-rise buildings, especially residential structures. In fact, the most livable and vibrant downtown districts throughout the world have a combination of new and old buildings. This synergy between the old and the new creates an upscale environment in which the new construction can command high rent, and thus pay for the cost of this top-end building. The retail and residential tenants of these historic properties get to enjoy the best of both worlds: an old building with great character updated with all the modern amenities.

Although the dominant trend still driving new construction favors the modern mindset—cheap, quick, and easy—times are changing. Historic city centers are coming back to life in many of our cities, and driving up real estate values. In Seattle, Portland, and Vancouver, British Columbia, for instance, the downtown areas with the largest volume of historic renovated buildings bring in the highest rent and sale price per sq. ft. of any property in the city. This trend also holds true for our smaller cities. The reason for this is largely because old buildings were designed on a pedestrian scale with retail shops at street level. These historic elements conform to a functional design that never goes out of style.

From an economic standpoint, one of the most important benefits to preserving these old buildings is their reuse value. With new construction, most of the cost of a project goes into the materials purchased and delivered to the site from outside the area. Whereas in rehabilitating old buildings, most of the original materials are recycled in place. The overall cost of a rehabilitation compared with constructing a new building of comparable size adds up to about the same amount. But here is an important difference: about 75% of the cost of rehabilitation comes in the form of labor. With new construction, about 75% of the budget is invested in construction materials. As the price of these materials continues to climb, the relative cost of new construction in comparison with rehabilitation favors the latter. We also must not overlook the strain that the production of new construction materials puts on the environment, from the extraction of raw materials from the earth to the energy consumed to fuel the production.

Revitalizing our urban communities by restoring old buildings is a pledge for a more sustainable future, and a return to a more human-scaled, community-oriented lifestyle. When the old buildings in our central business districts are converted for retail/residential use, our cities once again become vibrant and inviting cultural centers. Tenants and residents of historic buildings take pride in living and working in a place that gives them a sense of a shared cultural heritage. Young professionals and retirees alike enjoy the "twenty-minute lifestyle," as my son Kane refers to it—living within walking or biking distance of workplaces, restaurants, markets and entertainment. Scaled-down living has great appeal as well for "green-minded" citizens who want to reduce their footprint.

These old buildings were originally built to last hundreds of years and live through many generations of ownership. When we take over the ownership of a historic building, it means taking responsibility for the careful stewardship of the building over the course of its long life span. Those of us who purchase them are essentially just a series of caretakers in the life of these buildings. Hopefully, those of you who see the great potential for investing in this real estate will pass the buildings on to the next generation in an even better condition than when you first adopted them.

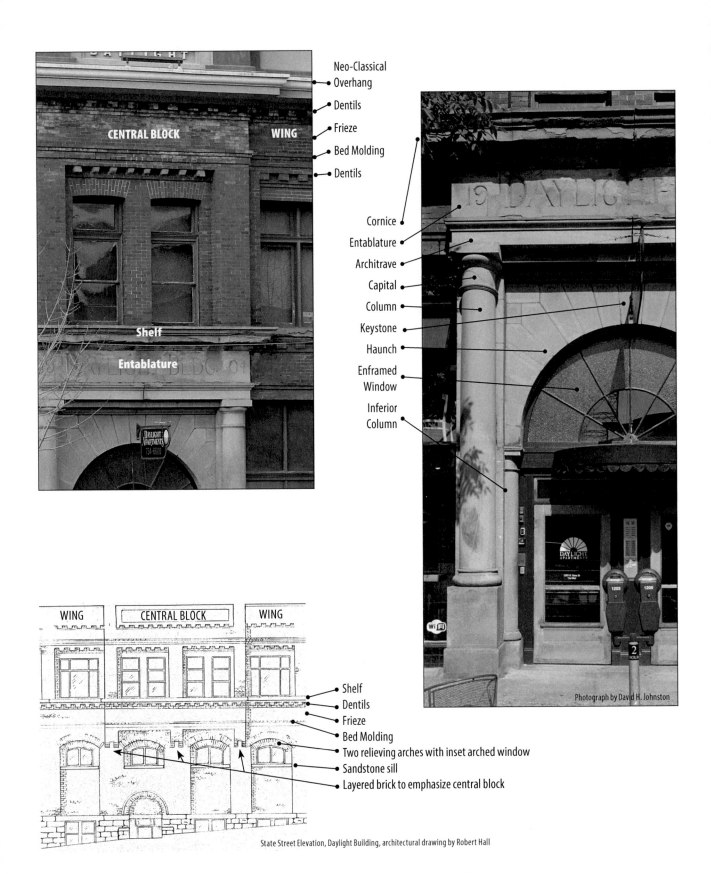

Neo-Classical Overhang
Dentils
Frieze
Bed Molding
Dentils

CENTRAL BLOCK   **WING**

Shelf

Entablature

Cornice
Entablature
Architrave
Capital
Column
Keystone
Haunch
Enframed Window
Inferior Column

Photograph by David H. Johnston

WING   CENTRAL BLOCK   WING

Shelf
Dentils
Frieze
Bed Molding
Two relieving arches with inset arched window
Sandstone sill
Layered brick to emphasize central block

State Street Elevation, Daylight Building, architectural drawing by Robert Hall

Glossary

ADA Standards: The Americans with Disabilities Act (1990) enforced accessible design standards for new buildings. Buildings pre-dating ADA regulations must be brought up to code when being renovated, if at all possible.

As-built: a technical term for what a building looks like in the present to compare with the original drawings and assess the best way to renovate the building.

As-built drawings: graphic depictions of a building on paper or CAD that, in theory, reflect the actual construction of every part and system of a building.

Building Code: a local statute that governs the design and construction of buildings. In most jurisdictions, building codes require a Certificate of Occupancy (CO) before a building can be legally occupied.

CAD (Computer Aided Drafting): software enabling the execution of drawings on a computer to a higher degree of accuracy than possible by hand.

Capital driven v. Market driven: An example of a capital driven landlord would be someone with an empty building who is unwilling to lower the stated rent, as this would decrease the appraised value; a market driven landlord would keep lowering the rent until it was leased.

Clearstory: a window design featured in old buildings, often located above the front entrance, that allowed daylight into the building.

Common Area: In commercial properties, fully enclosed space in a building, such as hallways and bathrooms, that benefits others in the building but does not accommodate tenant's furniture, etc.

Conduit: the small metal pipes externally mounted on the walls through which wires are pulled.

Cornice: the horizontal decorative molding that crowns a building, a door or window.

Discovery: slang word for the discovery of an issue that needs to be dealt with in a building rehab. It's best to find the issue before the purchase of a building during the inspection process, rather than to be surprised during the renovation.

Escrow money: money held by a neutral third party during a transaction between a buyer and seller.

Façade: an exterior side of a building, usually the front. The front of the building is most important from a historic preservation standpoint as it sets the tone for the rest of the building.

Floor plan: a scaled graphic representation of a horizontal section looking down through a building.

Footprint: the area enclosed by the building perimeter at the ground level of the building.

Gross sq. ft. vs. rentable sq. ft.: Gross area: the total of all areas of a building. Rentable Square Footage (RSF): the area of a building, floor or unit used as the basis for calculating base rent.

Grade: the surface of the ground at the outside face of the exterior enclosing wall.

Hung or dropped ceiling: a secondary ceiling hung below the main structural ceiling. Modern construction created the hung ceiling to hide the infrastructure (piping, wiring and ductwork).

Joist: one of the horizontal supporting members that run between foundations, walls, or beams to support a ceiling or floor.

Jump clause: term used for a flexible lease arrangement which allows the tenant and landlord to terminate the lease after giving at least 60 days notice.

Lath and plaster: a building process used for finishing interior walls and ceilings before the use of drywall and plasterboard in the 1950s. Wood laths, narrow strips of wood, are nailed across the wall studs or ceiling and plaster is applied over the lath.

Leveraging your cash: buying up as much property as possible with as little cash outlay up front as possible.

Mixed-use development: a commercial property that accommodates different uses, usually residential and retail.

National Register of Historic Places (NRHP): the federal government's official list of districts, sites, buildings, and structures deemed worthy of preservation. A property listed on the NRHP may qualify for tax incentives from expenses incurred preserving the property.

Net bottom line: Actual cash made.

Net Operating Income (N.O.I.): The net money a property makes exclusive of the mortgage payment.

Parapet: a low horizontal wall, often with an attached ledge, along the roof of a building.

Phase 1 Environmental Inspection: Banks require a Phase 1 inspection on commercial property to locate any asbestos, buried oil, or gas before they place a loan on it.

Profit and Loss (P & L) statement: the P & L statement is used to arrive at the value an appraiser puts on the property.

Pro forma: a financial projection of income and expenses used as a basis for securing financing for a property.

Red-tag: the designation for a structure that has been severely damaged to the degree that it is too dangerous to inhabit; discovery of work being done to a building without a valid permit. Government building officials perform tagging.

Scope creep: term used to describe the tendency of a project to expand as "discoveries" are made, requiring additional steps in the remodeling to bring a building up to regulation codes.

Stabilized: a building is considered stabilized after the rehab is finished and it is fully rented. This is the point when it is ready to be refinanced and the costs of the rehab paid back.

Stud wall: a stud is a vertical framing member in a building wall; used for partitions and for windows, doors, interior siding, etc.

Tenant Improvement (T.I.): the changes to a space that need to be done in order for the tenant to move in. Sometimes paid for by the tenant or the landlord. If done by the landlord, it is customary for the cost to be blended into the rent over the length of the lease.

Timber frame construction: a traditional method of constructing buildings with heavy structural wood beams and joints, making the architecture strong and durable; built to last.

Triple-net lease: Usually this includes the utilities, the real estate tax, common area expenses such as hallways and bathrooms, and general building maintenance such as boiler and roof.

Under contract: the buyer and the seller sign a contract that is binding to the seller but not the buyer until he or she removes the inspection and financing contingencies.

Vacancy Rate: the amount of rentable area that is truly vacant (not including leased unoccupied space) divided by the total rentable area in a building or group of buildings.

Working drawings: graphic depiction of a building on paper or CAD, prepared as the basis for a construction contract.

Photograph courtesy of Whatcom Museum.

About the Author

ROBERT K. HALL is a pioneer in the restoration and preservation of old commercial properties. For over 25 years, Hall has been on a mission to rescue old buildings from demolition and take them back to their original glory.

Hall's company, Daylight Properties, owns and manages more than 30 heritage buildings in the state of Washington. Hall is recognized in Bellingham as a foundation laying force in the revitalization of the historic downtown. Hall's historic restorations, including award-winning façade renovations, are recognized on the Washington Heritage Register and the National Register of Historic Places. Hall and his management team share a vision to preserve and showcase historic buildings by establishing healthy, sustainable businesses, and well-managed residential housing.

Made in the USA
San Bernardino, CA
15 June 2017